A World Bank Glossary

Glossaire de la Banque mondiale

*Glosario del Banco Mundial*

# Borrowing and Lending Terminology

## Terminologie des emprunts et des prêts

## *Terminología de empréstitos y préstamos*

English—French—Spanish

Français—anglais—espagnol

*Español—inglés—francés*

The World Bank
Washington, D.C., U.S.A.

International Bank for Reconstruction
and Development / The World Bank
Banque internationale pour la reconstruction
et le développement / Banque mondiale
Banco Internacional de Reconstrucción
y Fomento / Banco Mundial

1818 H Street, N.W.
Washington, D.C. 20433, U.S.A.



First printing November 1984
Première édition: novembre 1984
Primera impresión: noviembre de 1984
Second printing December 1985
Seconde édition: décembre 1985
Segunda impresión: diciembre de 1985

Manufactured in the United States of America
Publié aux Etats-Unis d'Amérique
Hecho en los Estados Unidos de América

**Library of Congress Cataloging in Publication Data**
Main entry under title:

Borrowing and lending terminology.

(A World Bank glossary = Glossaire de la Banque mondiale = Glosario del Banco Mundial)
"Prepared by the Terminology Unit of the World Bank's Language Services Division"—Foreword.
1. Loans, Foreign—Dictionaries—Polyglot. 2. Debts, External—Dictionaries—Polyglot. 3. Dictionaries, Polyglot. 4. World Bank—Language—Glossaries, etc. 5. International Finance Corporation—Language—Glossaries, etc. I. World Bank. Language Services Division. Terminology Unit. II. Title: Terminologie des emprunts et des prêts. III. Title: Terminología de empréstitos y préstamos. IV. Series.
HG3891.5.B65 1984 336.3'435'03 84-25684

ISBN 0-8213-0365-1

# Contents—Table des matières—*Indice*

**Foreword** v

Avant-propos **vi**

*Prefacio* **vii**

**Borrowing and Lending Terminology** 3
**English**—French—*Spanish*

Terminologie des emprunts et des prêts 33
Français—**Anglais**

*Terminología de empréstitos y préstamos* 47
*Español*—**Inglés**

# Foreword

The World Bank consists of the International Bank for Reconstruction and Development (IBRD) and its affiliate, the International Development Association (IDA). The International Finance Corporation (IFC) is also an affiliated institution of the IBRD.

This glossary contains terms which have appeared or may appear in documents dealing with lending and borrowing of the World Bank and IFC. Many of the terms are connected with IBRD's borrowing program, which has recently been under scrutiny within the Bank, in order to increase the sources of borrowing. As a result, many different financial instruments have been considered, and it is these that form a large part of this glossary.

Inevitably, the IBRD has been looking to the two major world financial markets, namely the U.S. and Eurodollar markets—so many of the terms will be unique to these two areas. As the language of these two markets tends to be mainly English, there are frequently no exact equivalents in French and Spanish, and many of the terms given should be considered as proposed translations and not standard terms. Naturally, where there is an equivalent used in French or Spanish, or where the experts in France or Spain and Latin American countries have an agreed term, it has been used. It should be noted, however, that many of these terms will be used in English by the experts, even when there is an accepted equivalent in French or Spanish. Definitions have been given for many of the terms. These are based on the English term, except where otherwise noted, and appear in the English section.

Besides terminology used in the financial markets, this glossary also contains terms relating to the World Bank's current lending program, including the currency pool and the pool-based lending rate (which are not the same thing), banking, accounting, particularly ratios, as well as a few terms in the fields of economics and financial analysis. The names of the United States and the United Kingdom have been consistently abbreviated to "U.S." and "U.K."

This glossary has been prepared by the Terminology Unit of the World Bank's Language Services Division. The Terminology Unit gives special thanks to the following staff members for their assistance: Carlos Castaño, Carmen Etcheberry-Freund, Gladys Murillo, Lianne Faili, Annie Malroux, Daniel Jimenez, Dominique Phung, and Nadia Rathier.

Any comments, including proposals for new terms and suggested alternative translations, will be most welcome and should be addressed to:

Terminology Unit
Language Services Division
The World Bank
1818 H Street, N.W.
Washington, D.C. 20433, U.S.A.

# Avant-propos

L'expression "Banque mondiale" désigne la Banque internationale pour la reconstruction et le développement (BIRD) et l'Association internationale de développement (IDA), qui lui est affiliée. La Société financière internationale (SFI) est également une institution affiliée à la BIRD.

Nous avons réuni dans le présent glossaire des termes rencontrés dans les documents relatifs aux prêts et aux emprunts de la Banque mondiale et de la SFI. Beaucoup de ces termes se rapportent au programme d'emprunt de la BIRD qui, soucieuse de se ménager de nouvelles sources de financement, a été amenée depuis peu à s'intéresser à de nombreux instruments financiers.

Il était inévitable que, pour élargir son programme d'emprunt, elle s'oriente vers les deux principaux marchés mondiaux de capitaux, ceux des Etats-Unis et des eurodollars, qui ont souvent leur propre terminologie, essentiellement anglaise. Bien des traductions que nous donnons ne doivent donc être considérées que comme de simples suggestions. Naturellement, chaque fois qu'il existe un équivalent accepté en français ou en espagnol ou que des experts de pays francophones ou hispanophones se sont mis d'accord sur un terme, nous l'avons repris. Il faut toutefois signaler que même s'il existe une traduction acceptée en français ou en espagnol, les experts emploient fréquemment le terme anglais. Nous avons généralement donné une définition qui, sauf indication contraire, est celle du terme anglais.

Outre le vocabulaire employé par les spécialistes des marchés financiers, ce glossaire contient des termes relatifs au programme de prêt de la Banque mondiale, notamment au pool de monnaies et au pool d'emprunts utilisé pour déterminer le taux prêteur (deux notions différentes), aux opérations bancaires, à la comptabilité (ratios par exemple) et même à l'économie et à l'analyse financière. Les sigles "U.S." et "U.K." ont été employés systématiquement pour désigner les Etats-Unis d'Amérique et le Royaume-Uni.

Ce glossaire a été établi par le Service de terminologie de la Division des services linguistiques de la Banque mondiale, qui tient à remercier particulièrement pour leur concours Carlos Castaño, Carmen Etcheberry-Freund, Lianne Faili, Daniel Jimenez, Annie Malroux, Gladys Murillo, Dominique Phung et Nadia Rathier.

Toutes les suggestions qui permettront d'améliorer et de compléter ce glossaire seront les bienvenues. Prière de les envoyer à l'adresse suivante :

Terminology Unit
Language Services Division
The World Bank
1818 H Street, N.W.
Washington, D.C. 20433, U.S.A.

# Prefacio

El Banco Mundial está constituido por el Banco Internacional de Reconstrucción y Fomento (BIRF) y su afiliada, la Asociación Internacional de Fomento (AIF). La Corporación Financiera Internacional (CFI) es también una institución afiliada del BIRF.

Este glosario contiene términos que han aparecido o pueden aparecer en documentos sobre operaciones de empréstito y préstamo del Banco Mundial y la CFI. Muchos de los términos están relacionados con el programa de empréstitos del BIRF, que recientemente ha sido objeto de un examen cuidadoso dentro del Banco con el fin de ampliar las fuentes de obtención de fondos. Como consecuencia, se han considerado numerosos instrumentos financieros distintos, y son éstos los que constituyen una gran parte del presente glosario.

Como cabía prever, inevitablemente el BIRF se ha dirigido a los dos principales mercados financieros del mundo—el de los Estados Unidos y el del eurodólar—, de modo que muchos de los términos corresponden a expresiones que se usan exclusivamente en dichos mercados. Dado que el idioma que se emplea en estos dos mercados generalmente es el inglés, con frecuencia no se encuentran equivalentes exactos en español y francés, por lo que muchas de las traducciones que se dan deben considerarse como sugerencias y no como términos consagrados. Lógicamente, en los casos en que se emplea un equivalente en español o francés, o en que los expertos de España y los países latinoamericanos o Francia tienen un término convenido, se ha usado éste. No obstante, cabe señalar que los expertos usarán muchos de estos términos en inglés, aun cuando exista un equivalente aceptado en español o en francés. En muchos casos se dan las definiciones. Salvo indicación contraria, éstas se basan en el término inglés y aparecen en inglés en la sección trilingüe.

Además de la terminología usada en los mercados financieros, este glosario contiene términos relacionados con el programa actual de operaciones crediticias del Banco Mundial, incluidos los referentes al fondo común de monedas, el tipo de interés variable basado en una "cesta" de empréstitos pendientes, banca, contabilidad—en particular relaciones—y algunos términos que se emplean en los campos de la economía y el análisis financiero. A través de todo el glosario los nombres de los Estados Unidos y el Reino Unido se han abreviado como "U.S." y "U.K.".

Este glosario ha sido preparado por la Dependencia de Terminología de la División de Servicios Lingüísticos del Banco Mundial. La Dependencia de Terminología expresa su agradecimiento en especial a los siguientes funcionarios por su asistencia: Carlos A. Castaño, Carmen Etcheberry-Freund, Lianne Faili, Daniel Jiménez, Annie Malroux, Gladys Murillo, Dominique Phung y Nadia Rathier.

Cualquier comentario, inclusive sugerencias relativas a la inclusión de nuevos términos o a traducciones distintas de las que aparecen en el glosario, será bien recibido. Las comunicaciones deben dirigirse a:

Terminology Unit
Language Services Division
The World Bank
1818 H Street, N.W.
Washington, D.C. 20433, U.S.A

*Borrowing and Lending Terminology*

English—French—*Spanish*

# - A -

**AAA bond** [cf., *top-rated bond*]
obligation de premier ordre; obligation (cotée) AAA (marché américain)
*bono, obligación (con clasificación) AAA*
Bond given highest rating in the *Standard & Poor* classification. AAA bonds have the highest degree of protection as regards principal and interest. The other main rating agency, *Moody's*, has Aaa as its highest rating. IBRD bonds are rated AAA.

**"A" loan**
prêt "A"
*préstamo "A"*
Standard World Bank loan in cofinancing.

**acceptance, accepting house** [U.K.]
maison d'acceptation
*casa de aceptaciones*
Merchant banks in the U.K. specializing in accepting bills of exchange.

**accounting price**
prix comptable
*precio de cuenta*
A price used for accounting purposes (i.e., not a market price). Often used synonymously with shadow price.

**accounting rate of interest (ARI)**
taux d'intérêt comptable (TIC)
*tasa de interés de cuenta (TIC); tipo de interés de cuenta (TIC)*
Discount rate used to convert future values of benefits and costs into equivalent present values.

**accounting ratio**
ratio prix comptable–prix du marché
*relación de cuenta*
Ratio of accounting price to market price of a good.

**accreted call bond**
obligation assortie d'une option d'achat au-dessous du pair
*bono redimible con descuento antes de su vencimiento*
Discount bond which allows the issuer to call the bond before maturity, at a discount from the face value.

**acid-test, liquid, quick ratio**
ratio de trésorerie réduite
*relación activo disponible-pasivo corriente*
The standard IBRD definition is the ratio of cash plus marketable securities plus accounts receivable plus other amounts readily convertible into cash to current liabilities. Other definitions include ratio of current assets less inventories to current liabilities, ratio of quick assets to current liabilities, ratio of cash plus near-cash assets to current liabilities, and ratio of cash plus accounts receivable plus the market value of selected investments to current liabilities. In Latin America, *relación de prueba ácida* is often found, while in Spain *ratio de tesorería* is used.

**activity ratios**
taux d'activité
*relaciones de actividad*
A group of ratios that measure movement in the activities of a corporation.

**actuarial evaluation**
évaluation actuarielle
*evaluación actuarial*

**advanced refunding**
refinancement anticipé
*refinanciamiento anticipado*
Refinancing before maturity, to take advantage of favorable market conditions.

**after-market**
après bourse
*período "after-market"*
The period between the issue of the security and lifting of syndicate restrictions in the fixed-interest and Eurobond markets. Sometimes used incorrectly as a synonym for *secondary market* (q.v.).

**after-sight bill**
traite à un certain délai de vue
*letra a cierto plazo de la fecha de presentación*
Bill of exchange which becomes payable at a certain date after presentation for acceptance.

**agency fee** [Euromarket]
commission de gestion
*comisión de gestión*

**agency securities, obligations**
obligations émises par des organismes fédéraux
*títulos de organismos federales; emisiones de organismos federales*
Security issued by a U.S. federal agency.

**agent bank**
1. correspondant; 2. mandataire; agent
*1. banco corresponsal; 2. banco agente*
1. Bank acting for a foreign bank. 2. Bank handling administration of loan in a syndicated credit.

**agio**
agio
*agio*
The premium which the metallic or other currency of a country may command over legal tender paper money which is its face equivalent.

**allotment**
attribution; répartition
*distribución*
Allocation of securities to members of the syndicate involved in the issue, in the Eurobond and U.S. securities market.

**all-purpose bank,** *see* combined commercial and investment bank

**amortization**
amortissement; remboursement [prêts]
*1. amortización; 2. depreciación*
1. The gradual extinguishment of any amount over a period of time (e.g., the retirement of a debt). 2. A reduction of the book value of a fixed asset.

**amortization adjustment factor** [currency pool]
facteur d'ajustement de l'amortissement
*factor de ajuste para fines de amortización*
The ratio of the current value, in terms of the U.S. dollar, of the principal outstanding of a loan at the commencement of business of a day to the corresponding total of withdrawals from the Loan Account, net of recalls for amortization.

**annuity bond**
titre de rente
*bono perpetuo, de renta vitalicia*

**apex loan**
prêt pyramidal, en cascade
*préstamo en pirámide, en cascada*
Loan whereby IBRD lends money to an apex development financial unit which onlends it to participating financial institutions which, in turn, onlend it to industrial companies.

**arbitrage**
arbitrage
*arbitraje*
Buying (or borrowing) in one market and selling (or lending) in another.

**arbitrageur**
arbitragiste
*arbitrajista*
Person systematically engaged in arbitrage dealing.

ARI, *see* accounting rate of interest

**arm's length (price)**
(prix) normal du marché; (prix) de pleine concurrence
*precio de mercado*
Price between corporations under fully competitive conditions (the opposite of *transfer price*).

**ask(ed) price [securities market]**
cours de l'offre
*precio vendedor*
The price at which a security or commodity is quoted or offered for sale.

ATM, *see* automatic teller machine

**automatic teller machine (ATM)**
guichet automatique de banque (GAB)
*ventanilla automática; cajero automático, permanente*

**availability clause,** *see* switch clause

**aval**
aval
*aval*
Guarantee of the payment of a bill of exchange or promissory note with the signature of a third person appearing on the bill.

**averaging**
amélioration des prix moyens (d'un titre)
*inversión periódica de monto constante*
The practice of investing a fixed amount of money in a particular security, regardless of price. When the market price is high, the investor receives proportionally less stock and vice versa.

# - B -

**"B" loan**
prêt "B"
*préstamo "B"*
Loan made by the World Bank involving cofinancing.

**back-to-back (loan, borrowing)**
1. échange de monnaies différentes; 2. (crédit) adossé; 3. (crédit) face à face; 4. opération couplée d'emprunts; emprunt de contrepartie
*1. préstamos cruzados en divisas; 2. crédito con garantía de otro crédito; 3. préstamo con intermediación de un banco; 4. empréstito de contrapartida*
1. Operations whereby a loan is made in one currency in one country against a loan in another currency in another country (e.g., a U.S. dollar loan in the U.S. against a pounds sterling loan in the U.K.). 2. A credit opened by a bank on the strength of another credit (e.g., if a British merchant buys cotton in Egypt and sells it to a Belgian who establishes a credit for payment to the U.K. firm, then the firm may be able to use this as a security for opening a credit to finance payment to the Egyptian.) 3. A scheme whereby a bank brings together a borrower and a lender so that they agree on a loan contract. 4. Refers to a variable-rate loan made by IFC to a borrower, for which the funds are borrowed from the IBRD. Also called *matched funding.*

**back-up line of credit**
ligne de crédit de protection, de soutien, auxiliaire
*línea de crédito de apoyo*

**backwardation**
déport
*1. situación en que el precio al contado es superior al precio a plazo; 2. prima pagada por aplazamiento de entrega*
1. In the commodity market, when the cash price is higher than the forward price. 2. In the stock exchange market, a charge paid by an investor who has not yet acquired securities, does not want to do so at the prevailing rate, and, therefore, does not take up delivery of the securities but carries delivery over to the next accounting period. (The opposite of *contango.*)

**backwardation rate**
intérêt de déport
*tipo de interés pagado por aplazamiento de entrega*

**balance-sheet ratio**
ratio tiré du bilan
*relación derivada del balance general*
Ratio based on figures appearing in the balance sheet.

**balloon loan**
prêt ballon
*préstamo "balloon"; préstamo amortizable en su mayor parte al vencimiento*
A loan repayment scheme, under which the last repayment is larger than the previous repayments. In some cases, the term is used to refer to a scheme, under which the whole loan is repaid at maturity.

BAN, *see* bond-anticipation note

**bank bill**
acceptation de banque
*pagaré bancario; letra bancaria*
Commercial bill accepted by a bank.

**banker's acceptance**
acceptation de banque
*aceptación bancaria*
U.S. and Canadian term for a bill of exchange which has been accepted by a banker.

**banker's draft**
chèque banque; chèque tiré
*letra de banco; cheque de banco*
A draft payable on demand and drawn by, or on behalf of, a bank upon itself.

**bank money**
monnaie scripturale
*depósitos bancarios*
Money on deposit at a bank.

**bank quality bond**
obligation pouvant intéresser les banques
*bono de calidad bancaria*
Bonds rated in the top four categories (AAA, AA, A, and BBB) and generally regarded as eligible for bank investment.

**bank trust departments**
services bancaires de gestion financière
*departamentos fiduciarios de bancos*

**basis point**
centième de pour cent; point de base
*centésimo de punto porcentual*
0.01 per cent of yield (e.g., of a security).

**bearer bond**
obligation au porteur
*bono, obligación al portador*
A bond whose title is to the bearer (i.e., it is presumed to be owned by its holder). The same as *coupon bond.*

**bearer market**
marché de porteurs
*mercado de títulos al portador*

**bearer note**
bon au porteur
*pagaré al portador*
Note where ownership is transferred merely by handing over, as opposed to registration.

**bearer scrip,** *see* scrip certificate

**bearer security**
titre au porteur
*título al portador*

**bellwether security**
titre précurseur
*valor precursor de tendencias*
A security that seems to lead a market movement or economic trend.

**best efforts sale**
vente sans garantie d'émission
*venta sin compromiso de garantía de emisión*
A new issue which is not underwritten and not purchased as a whole from the issuer, but is sold by securities dealers on a "sell what can be sold" basis. Used in the U.S. securities and syndicated Eurocredit markets.

**bid price**
cours acheteur
*precio comprador; precio de compra*
The price offered for a security or commodity by a prospective buyer.

**bill broker,** *see* discount house

**bill of exchange**
lettre de change
*letra de cambio*
An unconditional order in writing, addressed by one person to another, signed by the person giving it, requiring the person to whom it is addressed to pay on demand, or at a fixed or determinable future time, a sum of money to, or to the order of, a specified person or to bearer.

**blue chip**
placement de père de famille; valeur de père de famille; valeur de premier ordre
*valor de primera clase; acción de primera clase*
Share or security of top-rated U.S. corporation.

**bond**
obligation
*bono; obligación*
Debt instrument with maturity of longer than one year. Note that U.S. bonds are usually secured, while U.K. bonds and Eurobonds are usually unsecured.

**bond-anticipation note (BAN)**
avance de préémission
*pagaré en previsión de una emisión de bonos*
Short-term borrowing that serves as an interim source of funds for a project that is eventually to be financed by the sale of bonds.

**bond certificate**
certificat nominatif
*certificado nominativo*
Certificate given to the holder of a registered security.

**bondholder**
porteur de titres, d'obligations
*tenedor de bonos*

**bond-rating agency,** *see* rating agency

**bond sold on tap**
obligation vendue à guichet ouvert
*bono de venta continua*
A bond issued on an "as required" basis (i.e., it is continuously available and may be obtained on demand). The issuer may determine a maximum amount for the issue.

**bonus share**
action gratuite
*acción gratuita*
A share given as a bonus to purchasers of such shares.

**book-entry security**
titre relevé
*título consistente en un asiento bancario*
U.S. term for a security, not in the form of a certificate, but as an entry in an account at a bank. Eighty percent of marketable U.S. Treasury securities are now held in book-entry form.

**book value**
valeur comptable
*valor contable, en libros*
The net amount at which an asset appears on the books of account.

**border price**
prix frontière; prix franco frontière
*precio en la frontera; precio fronterizo*
Price of a tradable good at a country's border or port of entry.

**borrower's indebtedness subaccount [currency pool]**
sous-compte débiteur de l'emprunteur
*subcuenta de endeudamiento del prestatario*
Principal outstanding on a borrower's loan.

**borrow-pledge security loan**
prêt de titres garanti par d'autres titres
*préstamo en valores garantizado por otro(s) valor(es)*
Security loan where one or more securities are posted as collateral for the borrowed security.

**bought deal**
prise ferme
*emisión adquirida anticipadamente por un consorcio bancario*
Bond issue where a group of investment banks agree to purchase an entire issue for their own account or for resale, prior to announcing the issue to the market.

**break clause,** *see* jeopardy clause

**break-even point [stock market]**
niveau d'indifférence
*punto de equilibrio*
Point where two strategies are equivalent.

**broad money** [cf. M3]
monnaie, masse monétaire au sens large
*dinero en sentido amplio*

**broker**
[stock exchange] agent de change; agent boursier; [foreign exchange] courtier
*corredor (de cambio, de bolsa); agente (de cambio y bolsa)*

**broker loan rate**
taux d'avances sur titres
*tipo para préstamos con garantía de valores*
The rate banks charge to securities dealers and brokers on loans made with stock as collateral.

**brokerage**
courtage
*corretaje*

**Bruno ratio**
coefficient de Bruno
*relación de Bruno*
Also known as *domestic resource cost ratio* (q.v.).

**Bulldog bond**
obligation "bouledogue"; obligation étrangère émise à Londres
*bono "bulldog"*
Bond issued in pounds sterling on the London market outside the U.K.

**bullet issue**
emprunt remboursable en une seule fois; emprunt remboursable *in fine*
*préstamo reembolsable de una sola vez a su vencimiento*
An issue to be repaid in a lump sum at the end of its term rather than gradually.

**bunching (of maturities)**
concentration (des échéances)
*acumulación (de vencimientos)*

**buoyancy**, *see* tax buoyancy

**buy-back** [Canada]
prise en pension
*recompra*
A repurchase agreement in the Canadian short-term commercial market.

**buying rate** [securities market]
prix acheteur
*precio comprador*
The price that a buyer will pay for a security.

## - C -

**call-and-put option**, *see* straddle

**call loan**
prêt au jour le jour
*préstamo a la vista*
A loan on a demand basis (i.e., which either the borrower or lender may terminate at will).

**call money; day-to-day money; demand money; money at call**
argent au jour le jour; crédit à vue, à très court terme; avances à vue
*dinero exigible; dinero a la vista*
Money deposited in an interest-bearing account, that can be called by the depositor on a day's notice. Often applied to money lent by banks to stock exchange brokers, which may be called at any time.

**call-money rate**
taux de l'argent au jour le jour; taux des avances à vue
*tipo de interés para préstamos a la vista*

**call option**
option d'achat, de rachat
*opción de compra*
Option to purchase designated securities at a predetermined price within a specified time limit.

**call premium**
prime de remboursement
*prima de rescate*
The amount over the issue price when a bond is redeemed.

**call protection**
protection contre un rachat anticipé
*protección contra rescate anticipado*
Protection available in purchase of bonds, whereby a period is fixed during which the bond may not be redeemed.

**callable bond**
obligation remboursable avant l'échéance
*bono rescatable, redimible antes del vencimiento*
Bond with a call option.

**cancellation (of a debt)**
remise (d'une dette)
*condonación (de una deuda)*

**capital base**
assise financière; parfois, fonds propres
*base de capital*

**capital deepening**
approfondissement du capital
*aumento del capital con respecto al trabajo*
Action which increases the relative value of capital in relation to labor (cf. *capital widening*).

**capital-deepening investment**
investissement de productivité
*inversión orientada a aumentar la eficiencia de la producción y reducir los costos*
Investment aimed at increasing production efficiency and lowering costs.

**capital issue**
émission de titres
*emisión de valores de capital*

**capital market**
marché de capitaux; marché financier
*mercado de capitales*

**capital redemption reserve funds**
compte de réserves pour le rachat du capital des actions
*fondos de reserva para redención de capital accionario*
Special account held by a corporation to repurchase part of its shares.

**capital stock**, *see* equity capital

**capital widening**
élargissement du capital
*ampliación del capital*
Investment that increases the absolute value of capital (cf. *capital deepening*).

**capitalization**
capitalisation
*capitalización*
Total authorized par value of the stocks and bonds of a corporation.

**carry-over**
report de crédits
*saldo que pasa (al ejercicio siguiente)*
Funds unused during a financial year which are transferred to the budget for the following financial year.

**cash management**
gestion de (la) trésorerie
*gestión de caja, de liquidez*

**cash-management account**
compte de gestion de trésorerie
*cuenta de administración de fondos*
An interest-bearing current account, normally held with a stockbroker.

**cash-management bill**
bon du Trésor à très court terme
*bono del Tesoro (EE.UU.) a muy corto plazo*
Bill introduced by the U.S. Treasury in 1975, designed to raise funds quickly for a short period, ranging from nine to twenty days' maturity. Payment must be made in federal funds.

**cash market,** *see* spot market

**cash risk; liquid-holdings risk**
risque lié à la rentabilité des liquidités
*riesgo de liquidez*
Risk to actual cash receipts due to difference in spread between money borrowed medium term and reinvested short term.

**cash security loan**
prêt de titres garanti par des fonds
*préstamo de títulos con garantía en efectivo*
Security loan where cash is posted as collateral for the borrowed security.

**CD,** *see* certificate of deposit (CD)

**certificate of deposit (CD)**
certificat de dépôt
*certificado de depósito*
Certificate of an interest-bearing time deposit with a bank.

**changes in working capital statement,** *see* statement of changes in financial position

**chartered bank [Canada]**
banque à charte
*banco comercial*

**city bank [Japan]**
grande banque
*gran banco*
Major commercial bank, located in a city, dealing with corporations and major accounts (as compared to a local bank).

**clean**
(en) blanc; simple; non garanti
*sin garantía escrita*
Refers to a money market operation without underlying documentary security. (Note that in the U.K. *clean* means "exclusive of accrued interest.")

**clean advances**
avances non garanties
*anticipos sin garantía escrita*

**clean float**
flottement pur, non dirigé
*flotación limpia*
Floating of currency where the value of the currency is controlled by the market rather than the authorities. Opposite of *dirty float*.

**clearing agreement**
accord de compensation; accord de paiement
*acuerdo de compensación*

**clearing bank,** *see* investment bank

**clearing house**
chambre de compensation
*cámara de compensación*
An organization set up by financial institutions agreeing to initiate and receive among themselves electronic transfers of funds authorized by their customers.

**closed-end (investment) fund**
société d'investissement à capital fixe; société d'investissement fermée; fonds de placement fermé
*sociedad de inversión con número de acciones fijo*
U.S. term for an investment company with a fixed number of shares outstanding. The shares represent an interest in the fund's portfolio. New shares may not be issued.

**club loan**
crédit consortial (sans chef de file)
*préstamo concedido por un club bancario, por un consorcio*
Loan whereby, instead of one bank being designated lead bank and others comanagers or underwriters, the various functions these carry out are divided among the members, in order to save fees.

**colead manager,** *see* comanager

**coloan**
prêt cofinancé
*préstamo cofinanciado*

**comanager; colead manager**
co-chef de file
*banco codirector, coadministrador*
Lender ranking next to lead manager in a Euroloan.

**combined commercial and investment bank; multibank; all-purpose bank**
banque "multiservices", à tout faire, à vocation générale, polyvalente
*banco múltiple; multibanco [Chi., Mex.]*

**comfort**
sécurité
*garantía (dada por terceros)*
Security offered in a commercial loan in the form of a guarantee or cofinancing from a parent company, government, or international organization. See also *letter of comfort*.

**commercial bank; clearing bank [U.K.]**
banque de dépôt, commerciale
*banco comercial*

**commercial bills,** *see* commercial paper

**commercial lending**
prêts à des conditions commerciales
*préstamos en condiciones comerciales*
Lending not always at market rate but under normal market conditions (e.g., as regards maturity, reimbursement) (cf. *market-related lending*).

**commercial paper; commercial bills**
effets de commerce; papier commercial; papier financier
*efectos comerciales; papel comercial*
Promissory notes normally having a maximum maturity of 270 days sold by companies or institutions to raise cash for purposes of working capital. A major borrowing instrument for first-class borrowers in the U.S. and Canada.

**commissioned company [Japan]**
société mandatée (par la Banque mondiale pour la représenter à des émissions d'obligations au Japon)
*compañía comisionada; sociedad comisionada*
Agent in Japan which acts for the IBRD (or other non-Japanese financial institutions) in the issue of bonds on the Japanese market.

**commitment authority**
pouvoir d'engagement
*facultad para contraer compromisos*

**commitment fee; stand-by fee**
commission d'engagement
*comisión por compromiso, por inmovilización de fondos*

**common stock**
actions ordinaires; actions de capital
*acciones ordinarias*

**consol,** *see* nonmaturing, nonredeemable government bond

**consolidated discount notes**
bons à prime (d'émission) consolidés
*pagarés descontados consolidados*
Consolidation of several issues of discount notes into one uniform note.

**consumption rate of interest (CRI)**
taux d'actualisation de la consommation
*tasa de interés del consumo (TICO); tipo de interés del consumo (TICO)*
The rate at which the value of a unit of currency destined for consumption falls over time, usually expressed as an annual percentage.

**contango**
report
*"contango"*
In commodity markets, when the cash price is lower than the forward price. In the stock exchange market, the fee paid by an investor for the privilege of carrying the settlement of a transaction from one account period to another. (The opposite of *backwardation.*)

**contango rate; continuation rate**
intérêt de report
*interés de "contango"*
The difference between the cash and settlement prices.

**contingent obligation [IBRD]**
engagement conditionnel
*obligación contingente*
Type of IBRD "B" loan (q.v.) whereby the loan is initially financed entirely by the commercial lender with IBRD having a contingent commitment to finance at a given date (i.e., at the end of the duration considered "normal" by the commercial markets for the specific borrower) the remaining balance of principal (if any), if the commercial lenders choose not to finance this amount.

**continuation rate,** *see* contango rate

**contract financing**
financement sur contrat
*financiamiento con garantía de contratos*
Project finance, involving the use of commercial contracts such as a ship charter or take-or-pay contract as security for the loan.

**conversion discount**
décote de conversion
*descuento de conversión*
Ratio of the market value of a convertible security to its conversion value (q.v.) expressed as a percentage. When the market value of the security is lower than the conversion value, this ratio is said to be a discount.

**conversion premium**
prime de conversion
*prima de conversión*
Ratio of the market value of a convertible security to its conversion value (q.v.) expressed as a percentage. When the market value of the security is higher than the conversion value, this ratio is said to be a premium.

**conversion price**
prix de conversion
*precio de conversión*
The price which an investor must pay for a share, if he buys a convertible bond first and later converts it into shares.

**conversion value**
parité de conversion
*valor de conversión*
The conversion price multiplied by the current price of the security.

**core inflation**
inflation de base
*inflación básica*

**corporate bond**
obligation de société
*bono de una empresa privada, de una compañía, de una sociedad anónima*

**corporate right**
part sociale
*derecho (del accionista)*
Rights held by a partner in a corporation.

**country exposure**
engagement par pays
*compromisos por países*

**coupon**
coupon
*cupón*
A slip attached to a bearer bond, which can be detached and exchanged for an interest payment or dividend due at a specific date. Also used to describe the nominal annual rate of interest which a borrower promises to pay the holder of a fixed-income security. Colloquially, in the U.S. domestic market, used to describe a U.S. Treasury note or bond.

**coupon(-bearing) bond**
obligation munie de coupon
*bono con cupón*
Bond with coupon attached. Also called *bearer bond.*

**coupon equivalent yield**
rendement converti en taux d'intérêt
*rendimiento equivalente a un interés nominal*
The yield obtained from the difference between the purchase price and the face value of a short-term noninterest-bearing instrument, expressed as a percentage, determined by the difference divided by the purchase price.

**coupon note**
bon-coupon
*pagaré con cupón*
Note with coupon attached.

**coupon paper**
titres assortis de coupons
*títulos con cupón*
Paper with coupon attached.

**coupon rate**
taux de coupon
*interés nominal*
Interest to be paid regularly on the face value of a long-term debt instrument.

**creative financing**
formules nouvelles, inédites, originales de financement
*financiamiento innovador*

**credit standing; creditworthiness**
honorabilité [client privé]; surface financière; solvabilité; capacité d'endettement
*solvencia; solvencia crediticia*

**CRI**, *see* consumption rate of interest

**cross-currency interest hedge; double-hedge swap**
swaps portant à la fois sur les taux d'intérêt et sur des monnaies
*protección de "swap" doble*
Technique that combines shift from a floating to a fixed rate of interest, together with a shift from liability in one currency to liability in another.

**cross-default clause**
clause de manquement réciproque; clause d'exigibilité croisée
*cláusula recíproca en caso de incumplimiento*
A clause in a loan agreement specifying that default on any other loans to the borrower shall be regarded as default on this one.

**cross-over discount rate; equalizing discount rate**
taux d'indifférence; taux d'égalisation des valeurs actuelles
*tasa de actualización de equilibrio*
The discount rate that equalizes the net present value of two streams of benefits and/or costs.

**crowding-in**
attraction
*atracción*
Occurs where government bonds are sufficiently good money substitutes so that bond issues reduce demand for money balances, leading to an expansionary impact via their effect on portfolio composition.

**crowding-out**
éviction
*desplazamiento*
Any displacement of private economic activity by public economic activity.

**cumulative preferred stock**
actions cumulatives privilégiées
*acciones preferenciales, (preferentes, preferidas) acumuladas*
Preferred stock where the unpaid dividend is held over, totally or partially, when there are no returns in a financial year, or the returns are insufficient to distribute the dividend fixed for these shares.

**currency-linked bond**, *see* option bond

**currency option bond**, *see* option bond

**currency pool**
pool de monnaies
*fondo común de monedas*

**currency pooling system**
système du pool de monnaies
*sistema de fondo común de monedas*
A system set up by the World Bank to equalize among all borrowers, at any time, the risks inherent in fluctuations in the exchange rates of the currencies disbursed and repayable on all Bank loans included in the system. Equalization is achieved by pooling all currencies disbursed and outstanding on participating loans and by expressing the outstanding principal amount of each such loan as a share of the pool. As a result, loan-service obligations on each participating loan are related to all amounts in various currencies disbursed and outstanding on all loans in the system.

**currency swap**
swap de monnaies, sur le cours de change
*intercambio de monedas*
System whereby an institution with funds in one currency converts them into another and enters into a forward exchange contract to recover the currency borrowed.

**currency translation**
conversion monétaire; traduction monétaire
*traducción de monedas*
Recording in accounts of assets (or liabilities) in one currency when they are actually in another. No actual exchange of funds takes place. The World Bank and IFC, for example, translate all their assets and liabilities into U.S. dollar amounts, regardless of the actual currency in which they are denominated.

**current coupon (rate)**
taux de coupon courant
*interés nominal corriente*
1. In fixed-rate securities, a coupon rate which approximates current yield levels for similar securities. Straight debt securities with current coupons have prices close to par. 2. In floating-rate securities, the rate of interest on the current interest period.

**current ratio; working-capital ratio**
ratio de liquidité générale
*relación corriente [América Latina]; coeficiente de solvencia [Esp.]*
Ratio of current assets to current liabilities. It is the main liquidity ratio.

**cushion bond**
"cushion bond"
*bono amortiguador*
A high-coupon bond selling at a price above its call or optional redemption price.

**custom-duty bill**
obligation cautionnée
*letra aduanera garantizada*
Special type of credit in France granted by the state to corporations to allow them to pay indirect taxes or customs duty, with a guarantee provided by a bank or other financial institution. These bills allow the corporation to defer payment of value-added tax or customs duties. The state draws up a bill for the amount in question which the corporation agrees to pay on maturity.

## - D -

**day-to-day money**, *see* call money

**dealer [options market]**
agent de contrepartie
*agente de contrapartida*

**dealer [stock market]**
agent boursier; opérateur (sur le marché)
*agente de bolsa; corredor de bolsa*

**dealer [securities market]**, *see* securities dealer

**debenture (bond)**
1. obligation non garantie; 2. obligation
*1. bono sin garantía específica; debenture [Arg., Chile]; 2. bono con garantía de activos*
1. U.S.: Unsecured bond. 2. U.K.: Loan secured against specific or general assets of a company.

**debenture stock [U.S.]**
actions de priorité
*acciones privilegiadas*
A special type of stock conferring rights superior to both preferred and common stock. Note that in the U.K. *debenture stock* is the equivalent of the U.S. *debenture bond* (i.e., an unsecured bond).

**debt certificate**
certificat de reconnaissance de dette
*certificado de adeudo*
Loans against borrowers' notes, which are privately placed and can only be transferred by formal assignment.

**debt-equity ratio; debt-to-equity ratio**
ratio d'endettement
*relación deuda-capital; coeficiente de endeudamiento [Sp.]*
Mainly used to describe the ratio of total liabilities to shareholders' equity (net worth). It can also be used to describe the ratio of long-term debt to equity, net long-term debt to equity, total or long-term debt to tangible equity ( equity plus revenue plus capital reserves). All these definitions are used in the World Bank and IFC, so care should be taken in translation to ensure the correct term is used. Other definitions are used outside the World Bank.

**debt-for-debt swap**
swap sur des dettes
*intercambio de deudas*
Swap involving the exchange of a new obligation for an existing obligation held by investors. A technique used recently in the U.S. in conjunction with original-issue discount bonds (q.v.) as a means of realizing a capital gain on the retirement of a relatively low-coupon existing issue, and at the same time, achieving an interest cost saving due to special tax treatment of an original-issue discount bond issued as part of such a swap. New U.S. tax laws might well change this advantage.

**debt ratio**
ratio de solvabilité
*relación de endeudamiento*
Ratio of total liabilities to total assets.

**debt-service coverage**
couverture du service de la dette
*cobertura del servicio de la deuda*
Ratio of net income after taxes plus interest on long-term debt plus depreciation to debt service.

**debt-service ratio**
ratio du service de la dette
*relación del servicio de la deuda*
External public debt-service ratio (i.e., interest and principal payments) as a percentage of export earnings from goods, nonfactor services, and workers' remittances.

**debt-to-equity ratio,** *see* debt-equity ratio

**debt warrant**
warrant obligataire
*certificado para compra de bonos; "warrant" para compra de bonos*
Bond warrant, giving an investor the right to buy additional bonds at a predetermined price/yield.

**deep-discount bond, note**
obligation à prime d'émission élevée
*bono de descuento intensivo*
Bond with relatively low-coupon rate of interest, offered with a discount in excess of what can normally be treated as capital gain by the investor.

**demand money,** *see* call money

**depositary receipt**
titre en dépôt
*certificado de depositario*
A technique devised to permit trading in a security, even though the security does not fulfil the requirements for listing on the local stock exchange. A security is bought and registered in the name of the depositary bank or company, which will issue a receipt certifying that the receipt conveys the title to the security deposited with it or held to its order. If the receipt is in bearer form, it can then be freely bought and sold, whereas direct dealing in the stock would have needed registration of the new owner's name every time the security changed hands.

**detachable warrant**
warrant détachable
*certificado separable; "warrant" separable*

**dirty float**
flottement impur, contrôlé, dirigé, assisté, soutenu
*flotación impura, dirigida*
Floating of currency where the value of the currency is controlled by the authorities rather than the market. Opposite of *clean float.*

**disagio**
disagio; déport
*disagio*
Difference between nominal or par value and underlying market value.

**disaster clause,** *see* jeopardy clause

**discount [bills]**
escompte
*descuento*
Difference between price paid and face value of a bill or other paper.

**discount [bonds]**
prime d'émission
*descuento*
Difference between par value and purchase price of a bond.

**discount; markdown [foreign exchange]**
déport
*descuento*
In foreign exchange refers to a situation where currency can be bought more cheaply for a future date than for immediate delivery. For example, if US$1 buys FF 4 for delivery now, while it buys FF 5 for delivery twelve months hence,then the franc is said to be at a discount against the U.S. dollar.

**discount, to**
mobiliser
*descontar*
To discount a bill means to buy it for less than its face value, the difference between the price paid and the face value representing the implied rate of interest receivable by the purchaser, during the period before the bill is repaid.

**discount bond**
obligation à prime (d'émission)
*bono descontado*

**discount from par [securities market]**
décote
*descuento sobre el valor a la par*
Amount below face value at which a security is traded.

**discount house; bill broker**
maison de réescompte
*casa de descuento*
Intermediary between central bank and banking system, providing liquidity and ensuring the efficient operation of the money market. Does not exist in the U.S., but does exist in the U.K., France, South Africa, and Singapore. In the U.K., a discount house tends to be larger than a bill broker.

**discount note**
bon à prime (d'émission)
*pagaré descontado*
Note (i.e., short- or medium-term bond) issued at a discount from its face value. On maturity, the investor receives the full face value. The discount from par, thus, corresponds to the return on the investment.

**discount rate**
1. taux d'actualisation; 2. taux d'escompte
*1. tasa de actualización; 2. tipo de redescuento*
1. Annualized rate of discount applied to debt securities issued below par (e.g., U.S. Treasury bills). 2. Rate at which a central bank (Federal Reserve System in the U.S.) (re)discounts certain bills for financial institutions.

**discount window**
escompte officiel
*redescuento*
Rediscount facility offered by central bank (Federal Reserve System in the U.S.).

**discount without recourse**
escompte à forfait, en ducroire, sans recours
*descuento sin recurso*
Purchase of negotiable instruments where the buyer waives the right of recourse in respect of the seller of the instrument, to which the buyer would be entitled.

**disintermediation**
desintermédiation
*desintermediación*
1. Shift of funds away from financial intermediaries (commercial banks, etc.) into U.S. Treasury bills and other securities. 2. Shift by large corporations away from banks to a parallel market, involving other large corporations.

**distressed loan**
prêt en difficulté
*préstamo que se halla en dificultades*
Loan on which repayment of interest and principal has been severely delayed or completely suspended.

**dividend-right certificate**
bon de jouissance
*bono de usufructo*
Equity paper which does not confer any ownership rights (e.g., voting rights), but grants the holder the right to participate in the net profit and liquidation proceeds and the right to subscribe to new shares in the case of a rights issue.

**dividend-right share**
action de jouissance
*acción de usufructo*
Equity paper, issued in the place of repaid shares, conferring membership rights and the right to participate in the distribution of profits and liquidation proceeds of a corporation.

**dividend stock**
actions bénéficiaires
*acciones con derecho a dividendo*

**domestic resource cost (DRC)**
coût en ressources intérieures; coût réel des devises
*costo en recursos internos*
Cost of resources used in products that are not imported.

**domestic resource cost ratio**
coefficient de coût en ressources intérieures
*coeficiente de costo en recursos internos*
Ratio of the cost of all factors of domestic origin (evaluated at their opportunity cost) to the domestic added value (at world prices). Also known as *Bruno ratio* (q.v.).

**double hedge swap,** *see* cross-currency interest hedge

**double-weighted borrowing cost [IBRD]**
coût des emprunts doublement pondéré
*costo de los empréstitos con doble ponderación*
When calculating borrowings, the IBRD takes the amount of the loan, multiplies it by the interest rate, and obtains a total for the interest. All the loans are added and all the interest totals. The first sum is then divided by the second to obtain the weighted average interest. This is the single-weighted borrowing cost. Recently, the IBRD has obtained the interest total by multiplying the amount of the loan by the interest and the number of years to maturity, to take into account the fact that it has loans of varying maturities. The weighted averaged interest obtained from this calculation is called the double-weighted borrowing cost.

**DRC,** *see* domestic resource cost (DRC)

**drop lock**
clause "drop lock"; clause de verrouillage au taux plancher
*congelación del interés en un nivel mínimo (cuando la tasa de mercado desciende a menos de ese nivel)*
Clause in floating-rate note whereby, if market interest rates fall below a specified minimum, the rate of interest is fixed at that minimum and "locked" in for the remaining life of the loan.

**Dutch auction [U.S.]**
adjudication à prix uniforme
*adjudicación a precio uniforme; subasta a la baja*
A competitive bidding technique sometimes used in U.S. securities markets, whereby the lowest price necessary to sell the entire amount of securities offered becomes the price at which all securities are sold.

## - E -

**early redemption option bond,** *see* retractable bond

**economic price; efficiency price**
prix économique
*precio económico*
Price reflecting relative value to be assigned to inputs and outputs if the economy is to produce the maximum value of physical output efficiency.

**ECU,** *see* European Currency Unit (ECU)

**efficiency price,** *see* economic price

**EFT,** *see* electronic funds transfer (EFT)

**electronic funds transfer (EFT)**
transfert de fonds électronique
*transferencia electrónica de fondos*
System of transferring funds from one account to another by electronic impulses rather than transfer of paper (such as a check).

**equalizing discount rate,** *see* cross-over discount rate

**equity,** *see* stockholders' equity

**equity capital; capital stock (of a corporation)**
capital social
*capital social; capital accionario*
The issued share capital which is neither limited nor preferred in its participation in the distribution of its profits nor in the ultimate distribution of its assets. *Equity capital* is sometimes used as a synonym for *stockholders' equity* (q.v.).

**equity ownership**
participation au capital social d'une société
*participación en el capital social*

**EUA,** *see* European Unit of Account (EUA)

**Eurobond**
euro-obligation
*eurobono*
A bond issued in a currency other than that of the market or markets in which it is sold. The issue is handled by an international syndicate.

**Eurocommercial paper**
effets de commerce en eurodevises
*efectos comerciales en eurodivisas*
Commercial paper issued in a Eurocurrency.

**Eurocurrency**
euromonnaie; eurodevises
*euromoneda; eurodivisas*
A currency deposit held outside the country which issued the currency.

**Eurocredit**
eurocrédit
*eurocrédito*
Any lending made using Eurocurrency, generally a medium-term bank loan.

**Eurodollar**
eurodollar
*eurodólar*
A dollar deposit acquired by a person or bank not resident in the U.S. and held outside the U.S.

**Euroloan**
europrêt
*europréstamo*
A loan made using Eurocurrency

**Euromarket**
euromarché
*euromercado*
The Eurocurrency, Eurocredit, and Eurobond market.

**European Currency Unit (ECU)**
unité monétaire européenne (écu)
*unidad monetaria europea (ECU)*
A standard unit of account of European Community member countries.

**European Unit of Account (EUA)**
unité européenne de compte (uec)
*unidad de cuenta europea (UCE)*
A composite currency unit based on the value of the currencies of the European Community members participating in the European Monetary System.

**even par swap**
swap d'obligations à valeur nominale égale
*trueque de bonos de valor nominal igual*
U.S. term for the sale of one block of bonds and the simultaneous purchase of the same nominal principal amount of another block of bonds, without regard to the net cash difference.

**even roll**
refinancement pour un montant égal
*refinanciamiento de monto igual*
Refunding, where approximately the same amount of debt is being issued for the old debt.

**exercise price,** *see* striking price

**exposure**
risque; part des risques; engagement
*riesgo; préstamos pendientes*
Amount of investment made, with the additional idea of risk. These translations are proposed. The translation will often depend on the context, and the term cannot be easily translated by a word or short phrase.

**extendible bond; extendible-maturity bond**
obligation reconductible
*bono de vencimiento ajustable*
maturity bond

**extendible maturity bond,** *see* extendible bond

**extendible maturity note,** *see* extendible note

**extendible note; extendible-maturity note**
obligation reconductible
*pagaré de vencimiento ajustable*
maturity note

**extension fee**
commission de reconduction
*comisión de renegociación*
Supplementary fee payable to lender of a loan extended beyond original period.

**external bond issue**
émission d'obligations à l'étranger
*emisión de bonos en el exterior*
Issue of bonds in a foreign country.

## - F -

**face value,** *see* par value

**federal funds**
fonds fédéraux
*fondos federales*
Cash balance held by banks with local Federal Reserve bank. They are immediately

available (e.g., for transfer between banks). Note that *monnaie centrale* is the money held by a French bank at the *Banque de France* (central bank) and is the French equivalent of *federal funds*.

**federal funds rate**
taux des fonds fédéraux
*tipo de los fondos federales; tasa de los fondos federales*
Rate of interest paid on federal funds. Equivalent to interbank rate.

**federally chartered bank** [U.S.]
banque à charte fédérale
*banco con autorización federal*
A bank legally authorized to receive deposits.

**Federal Reserve System** [U.S.]
système fédéral de réserve
*Sistema de la Reserva Federal*
The central banking system of the U.S. It has twelve Federal Reserve Banks divided up by geographical regions. The Board of Governors supervises the operations of the regional banks and coordinates monetary policy through its Federal Open Market Committee.

**financial deepening**
augmentation de l'importance des circuits financiers
*intensificación financiera*
Acquisition of financial assets at a faster rate than nonfinancial assets.

**financial futures**
instruments financiers à terme
*instrumentos financieros a plazo*
Futures of bills, notes, bonds, currency, and commercial paper.

**financial intermediary**
intermédiaire financier
*intermediario financiero*
Normally, an intermediary between the U.S. Treasury (or equivalent) and the market.

**financial ratios**
ratios de structure; ratios financiers
*relaciones financieras*
Ratios which show a corporation's financial structure. They include liquidity and leverage ratios.

**financial repression**
répression financière
*represión financiera*
Distorsion in the financial system, with negative interest rates, subsidy interest rates to some privileged borrowers, selective credit allocation, and excessive bureaucratic control over the financial system.

**fine-tuning (of the economy)**
réglage de précision
*afinamiento (de la economía)*

**fiscal agent**
agent financier
*agente financiero*
A bank appointed by the borrower as its agent for a new issue of securities when no trustee has been appointed. Its functions include those of a principal paying agent and a number of the clerical functions but none of the fiduciary responsibilities of a trustee.

**fiscal drag**
1. érosion fiscale des revenus; 2. freinage fiscal
*1. lastre fiscal; rémora fiscal; 2. freno fiscal*
1. Reduction in real income due to the increase in income from inflation, resulting in income earners being placed in higher tax brackets. 2. Action by public financial authorities with regard to economic activity.

**fixing**
cotation (de la barre d'or); fixing
*cotización*
Quotation of the price of a bar of gold in the market.

**flat**
tel quel
*sin intereses*
Excluding accrued interest. A bond where the interest is included in the price is said to be traded flat ("une obligation négociée tel quel").

**float** [banking]
moyens de paiement à l'encaissement; moyens de paiement non recouvrés
*efectos en cobro, cobranza*
Checks, drafts, etc., in the process of collection.

**floating-rate bond**
obligation à taux flottant; obligation à taux variable (OTV)
*bono con interés variable*
Bond on which the coupon is established periodically and calculated with reference to short-term interest rates.

**floating-rate note (FRN)**
bon à taux flottant; bon à taux révisable
*pagaré con interés variable*
Note issued from five to fifteen years with a fixed spread, usually over the six-month London Interbank Offered Rate (LIBOR), normally with provision for a minimum interest rate. Primarily used by banks to raise dollars for their Euromarket operations.

**floor broker**, *see* floor trader (definition)

**floor rate of exchange**
taux de change minimum
*tipo de cambio mínimo*
The minimum rate of exchange.

**floor trader**
agent opérant directement sur le parquet
*corredor de bolsa independiente*
Member of an exchange trading for himself. Note that *floor broker* is a broker on the New York Stock Exchange who acts for other members of the Stock Exchange only.

**flow of funds**, *see* funds flow

**flow-of-fund table** [national accounts]
tableau d'opérations financières
*cuadro de corrientes financieras*
A table showing transactions in financial claims between institutional units.

**foreign-exchange warrant**
warrant en devises
*certificado en divisas; "warrant" en divisas; libranza en divisas*

**forfeiting**
forfaitage
*descuento de pagarés a mediano plazo*
The business of discounting medium-term promissory notes or drafts related to an international trade transaction. Repayments are semiannual and discounting is at a fixed rate.

**forward-forward arbitrage,** *see* time arbitrage

**forward market**
marché à terme
*mercado a plazo, a término, de futuros*

**founder's share**
part de fondateur; part bénéficiaire
*participación de fundador*

**fourth market**
quatrième marché
*cuarto mercado*
Market for large block sales of securities arranged by private firms.

**FRN,** *see* floating-rate note

**front-end fee**
commission d'ouverture
*comisión inicial*

**front-loaded spending**
dépenses groupées au début (d'une période donnée)
*gasto concentrado al comienzo de un período*

**full face value**
valeur nominale totale
*valor nominal*

**full, fully paid stock,** *see* paid-up stock

**funded debt**
dette consolidée
*deuda consolidada*

**funding latter maturities [IBRD]**
financement des dernières échéances
*financiamiento de los últimos vencimientos*
Type of IBRD "B" loan (q.v.), whereby IBRD would take an initial share of the loan up to about 25 percent, concentrated in the latter maturities.

**funding pro rata [IBRD]**
participation proportionnelle
*participación proporcional*
Type of IBRD "B" loan (q.v.), whereby IBRD takes a pro rata share of about 10 percent in each maturity of the commercial loan.

**funds flow; flow of funds**
flux financiers
*flujo de fondos; corriente de fondos*
The flow of purchasing power into and out of an organization. Inward flows include sales revenue, sales of fixed assets and investments, and issues of debentures, loans, and shares. Outward flows include purchases of fixed assets and investments, repayment of debt, payment of dividends, and taxation on profits.

**funds flow statement,** *see* statement of changes in financial position

**funds statement,** *see* statement of changes in financial position

**funk money,** *see* hot money

**futures [commodities market]**
opérations à terme
*futuros*

**futures, financial,** *see* financial futures

## - G -

**the gap [IBRD],** *see* overall risk profile

**gearing ratio,** *see* leverage ratio

**gearing ratio [IBRD]**
coefficient d'utilisation des fonds propres; rapport encours des prêts/fonds propres
*relación préstamos desembolsados y pendientes–capital y reservas*
Ratio of capital plus reserves to loans outstanding and loans disbursed.

**general-obligation bond,** *see* general obligations

**general-obligations; general-obligation bonds**
emprunts de collectivité locale
*bonos de responsabilidad general*
Long-term borrowings, usually by a municipality, that are backed by the full faith, credit, and taxing powers of the issuing locality rather than income generated by a specific project.

**Gensaki**
Gensaki
*Gensaki*
A Yen repurchase agreement.

**gilt-edged securities**
1. fonds d'Etat britanniques; valeurs garanties par l'Etat; 2. valeurs de premier ordre
*1. bonos del Gobierno británico; 2. valores de primer orden*
1. British Government bonds. 2. U.S. bonds of AAA standing.

**government debt instruments**
instruments de la dette publique
*instrumentos de la deuda pública*

**government paper**
effets publics
*efectos públicos*

**government-security dealer**
courtier en fonds d'Etat; courtier d'effets publics
*corredor de valores del Estado*

**grading,** *see* rating

**grey, gray market**
marché gris
*mercado gris*
Market in bonds that have not been been given a firm price.

**guarantee [IBRD]**
1. garantie de la BIRD; 2. garantie (de l'Etat)
*1. garantía; 2. garantía (del Estado)*
1. Type of IBRD "B" loan (q.v.) with IBRD guaranteeing part of the loan and offering the commercial colender a "put" on the latter maturities of the loan, which would represent an IBRD commitment to purchase the designated maturities at the request of the colender. 2. Loan made to a domestic corporation guaranteed by the state.

**guarantee commission, fee [IBRD]**
commission de garantie
*comisión de garantía*
Commission payable periodically (e.g., to IBRD) as compensation for the risk in guaranteeing a loan.

## - H -

**hedge [securities market]**
valeur de refuge
*valor de protección*
Security acquired to cover possible loss on speculative investments.

**hedging**
couverture des opérations à terme; opérations d'arbitrage en couverture d'actifs; opérations en countrepartie
*operaciones de cobertura, de protección cambiaria*
Purchase or sale of currency, usually on a forward basis, as a means of unsuring against loss should an exhange rate change.

**hot bill**
effet brûlant
*efecto a la vista o de vencimiento a muy corto plazo*
Bill which matures at sight or whose maturity is less than the period making possible its collection in good time, necessitating immediate presentation for payment.

**hot money; funk money [U.K.]**
capitaux fébriles
*capitales itinerantes*
Short-term international capital movements, motivated by interest rate differentials or revaluation hopes/devaluation fears.

**hung-up issue**
émission collée
*emisión empantanada; emisión atascada*
An issue which dealers have not managed to fully place.

**hurdle rate**
taux critique de rentabilité
*tasa crítica de rentabilidad*
A somewhat arbitrary rate of return, related to the current cost of borrowing money, set by a government or company to guide investment decisions. Below this limit, investment is normally considered inadvisable.

## - I -

**IBF**, *see* international banking facility

**imprest account, fund**
compte d'avances de caisse; compte d'avances temporaires
*cuenta de anticipos; fondo de anticipos*
An account or fund maintained for payments made in cash, commonly used as a petty cash fund. A fixed maximum sum is kept in the fund and, as the fund is depleted, this sum is periodically brought up to the maximum.

**income bond; participating bond**
obligation participante
*bono participatorio*
In the U.S., bonds which are guaranteed as to principal but which have interest payments as a contingent obligation, that are required only if earned and then assented to by the board of directors. Failure to pay interest does not constitute default. (Note that in the U.K., *income bond* refers to a type of fixed-interest investment offered by life insurance companies, consisting of an immediate annuity plus a deferred annuity.)

**indexed bond; index-linked bond**
obligation indexée
*bono ajustable, indizado*
Bond where the coupon rate or redemption value is indexed (to other currencies, gold, or fuel prices). Used in Brazil, Chile, Finland, France, Iceland, Israel, Sweden, and the U.K.

**indexed loan [currency pool]**
prêt indexé
*préstamo reajustado*
Loan indexed to the daily variation of the U.S. dollar value of the pool due to exchange rate fluctuation.

**index-linked bond**, *see* indexed bond

**inflation premium**
prime de risque-inflation
*prima por inflación*
A premium added to a security to allow for inflation.

**inside, insider dealing**
transactions d'initiés
*transacciones de personas iniciadas*

**instruments**
instruments; papiers
*instrumentos*

**interest-bearing notes**
effets porteurs d'intérêt
*pagarés que devengan intereses*

**interest-coverage ratio**
ratio de couverture de l'intérêt
*relación de cobertura de intereses*
Net income before interest expenses divided by interest expenses.

**interest leakage**
fluctuation des taux due à une fuite de capitaux
*fluctuación de los tipos de interés debida a la fuga de capitales*
Changes in U.S. interest rates due to movement of funds from the U.S. to the Eurodollar markets.

**interest-rate risk**
risque de perte sur les taux d'intérêt
*riesgo relacionado con los tipos de interés*
Risk due to difference in interest rates.

**interest-rate swap**
accord de swap sur les taux d'intérêt; swap de taux d'intérêt
*trueque de tipos de interés*
An agreement to exchange floating-rate payments for fixed-rate payments in the same currency.

**intermediation**
intermédiation
*intermediación*
Process whereby a financial institution interposes its names and trustworthiness between a lender and a borrower. For example, instead of buying an issue directly from a corporation, an investor may deposit funds with a bank which, in turn, invests in the issue.

**international banking facility (IBF)**
service bancaire international
*servicio bancario internacional*
International branch of a bank in a kind of internal free-trade zone in the U.S., which allows banks to engage in international banking without some of the usual restrictions facing domestic banks. Those restrictions from which IBFs are exempt include reserve requirements, payment of certain insurance premiums, and special relief from state tax.

**investment bank [U.S.]; merchant bank [U.K.]**
banque d'affaires
*banco de inversiones*
Institution that accepts new issues of stocks from a corporation and attempts to sell them to the public at a profit. In the U.S., they have a separate legal status from commercial banks.

**investment broker**
courtier en placements
*corredor de inversiones*

**investment company, fund**
société d'investissement; société de placement collectif
*compañía de inversiones; sociedad de inversiones; fondo de inversiones*
Corporation that functions as a financial intermediary between the public and the financial markets.

**investment securities**
titres de placement
*valores de inversión a largo plazo*
Securities that are particularly suitable for long-term investment (e.g., bonds). Also includes top-rated shares.

**inward swap**
mise en report
*recompra de divisas en moneda nacional*
Spot sale of foreign exchange and forward repurchase of same foreign currency against domestic currency.

**issuer**
organisme d'émission; émetteur
*emisor*

**issuing calendar**
calendrier des émissions
*calendario de emisiones*
Compulsory timetable for issue of new securities (Switzerland, Federal Republic of Germany).

## - J -

**jeopardy clause; disaster clause; break clause**
clause de sauvegarde
*cláusula de salvaguardia*
A clause in a Eurocurrency agreement specifying that, if certain events curtail the lender's activity or the operation of the Euromarkets, other designated actions will come into effect.

**jobber**
agent boursier opérant pour son propre compte; "jobber"
*agiotista*
A broker on the London Stock Exchange who acts on his own behalf.

**joint financing**
financement conjoint
*financiamiento conjunto*
Disbursement by two lenders for the same parts of the project in a fixed ratio.

**jumbo certificate of deposit**
certificat de dépôt d'un montant minimum de US$100.000
*certificado de depósito de US$100.000 o más*
Certificate of deposit of US$100,000 or more.

**jumbo borrowing**
emprunts géants
*empréstitos gigantescos*

**junior debt; subordinated debt**
dette de deuxième rang
*deuda subordinada*
A debt ranking below amounts owed to general creditors. Such an arrangement may be agreed to in the case of a financially embarassed debtor where a creditor has faith in the debtor's business future.

## - L -

**lag risk [IBRD]**
risque dû au décalage [à compléter selon le contexte]
*riesgo relacionado con un desfase*
1. Risk of lending at low interest rates and having to finance at high interest rates at a later date. 2. Risk run by IDA between the period of disbursement and receipt of commission.

**lead bank; lead manager**
chef de file; teneur de plume
*banco director*
Bank with main responsibility for arranging a bond issue or international Eurocredit. While *teneur de plume* can be the same as a *chef de file*, in a jumbo loan the *teneur de plume* will be the lead manager, even though there are several other *lead managers* (*chefs de file*) or colead managers (*co-chefs de file*). Lead manager is also used in the sense of *agent bank* (q.v.).

**lender of last resort**
prêteur en dernier ressort; prêteur de dernier recours
*prestamista de última instancia*

**letter of comfort**
lettre de confort
*carta de seguridades*
A written instrument issued by A, where A agrees to make every effort to assure B's compliance with the terms of a contract, but without committing A to perform B's obligation in the event that B is unable to fulfil his obligation. Usually issued by a parent company on behalf of a subsidiary in another country.

**level repayment**
remboursement en tranches égales
*reembolso en cuotas iguales*

**leverage (ratio) [U.S.]; gearing (ratio) [U.K.]**
ratio de levier; ratio de structure du passif; ratio de solvabilité-endettement
*nivel de endeudamiento relativo al capital; relación endeudamiento/capital propio*
Ratio of debt/liabilities to equity/assets. Includes debt and debt-equity ratios.

**liability management**
gestion du passif
*gestión del pasivo*

**LIBOR**
LIBOR
*LIBOR*
London Interbank Offered Rate. The interest rate at which banks in London are prepared to lend funds to first-class banks. It is used to determine the interest rate payable on most Eurocredits.

**limited-recourse finance**
financement avec droit de recours limité
*financiamiento con recurso limitado*
Finance arranged on the basis of the lender having recourse to the borrower only in certain circumstances (e.g., the loan to British Petroleum (BP) to finance the Forties oil field in the North Sea, where the lenders had no recourse to BP if there was insufficient oil).

**liquid-holdings risk,** *see* cash risk

**liquidity portfolio**
portefeuille liquide
*cartera líquida*

**liquidity premium**
prime de liquidité
*prima de liquidez*
A notional premium paid by borrowers to lenders to encourage them to lend money at a fixed rate in the long term, when interest rates are likely to rise and it is, therefore, more profitable to invest in short-term paper.

**liquidity ratios**
ratios de liquidité; coefficients de liquidité
*coeficientes de liquidez; relaciones de liquidez*
Ratios which reflect a borrower's ability to meet his short-term obligations. They include the acid-test ratio (q.v.) and the current ratio (q.v.).

**liquid ratio,** *see* acid-test ratio

**listed security**
valeur cotée en Bourse
*valor cotizado en bolsa*
An issue of a security accepted for trading on a stock exchange.

**load fund**
fonds qui prélève une commission
*fondo de inversión que cobra una comisión*
Mutual fund which charges a handling fee.

**loan portfolio**
portefeuille de prêts
*cartera de préstamos*

**loan syndicate,** *see* syndicate

**locked market**
marché figé
*mercado inmovilizado*
Market where bid and offer prices are exactly the same.

**lock rate**
taux plancher de verrouillage
*tasa de inmovilización*
Rate at which drop lock (q.v.) clause becomes operative.

**Lombard rate [Federal Republic of Germany]**
taux des avances sur titres; taux Lombard
*tipo Lombard*
German term for the rate of interest charged for a loan against the security of pledged paper. Particularly used with reference to the German Bundesbank, which normally maintains its Lombard rate at about 0.5 percent above its discount rate.

**long hedge**
opérations de couverture par achat à terme
*operaciones de cobertura por compra a plazo*
Hedging operation by someone who is "long" (i.e., who owns more than he has contracts to deliver).

**long-term debt ratio**
ratio d'endettement à long terme
*relación de endeudamiento a largo plazo*
Ratio of long-term debt to total assets.

**lump-sum borrowing [IFC]**
emprunt global
*empréstito de suma alzada*
A currency-specific borrowing made in a lump sum by IFC from IBRD for its short-term future needs.

## - M -

M1
M1
*M1*
In the U.S., notes and coins in circulation, demand deposits at all commercial banks other than those due to domestic banks, the U.S. Government, and foreign banks and official institutions, less cash items in the process of collection and Federal Reserve float; traveler's checks of nonbank issues; and negotiable order of withdrawal (NOW) and automatic transfer services (ATS), accounts at banks and trust institutions, credit union share draft accounts, and demand deposits at mutual savings banks. It is the narrow money supply. Definitions will differ from country to country.

**M2**
M2
*M2*
In the U.S., M1 plus savings and small-denomination time deposits at all depository institutions; overnight repurchase agreements at commercial banks; overnight Eurodollars held by U.S. residents other than banks at Caribbean branches of depository institutions; and the balance of money market mutual funds (general purpose and broker/dealer). Definitions will differ from country to country.

**M3**
M3
*M3*
In the U.S., M2 plus large-denomination time deposits at all depository institutions; term repurchase agreements at commercial banks and savings and loan associations; and balances of institution-only money market mutual funds. It is the broad money supply. Definitions will differ from country to country.

**maker (e.g., of a note)**
émetteur
*librador (p. ej. de un pagaré)*

**management fee**
1. commission de direction; commission syndicale; 2. commission de gestion; frais de gestion
*comisión de administración; comisión de gestión*
1. Fee charged by a bank for managing a credit or bond issue. 2. Fee charged for portfolio management.

**management, managing group [Eurodollar market]**
groupe de direction; syndicat de direction
*grupo de dirección*

**manager (of syndicate),** *see* agent bank

**managing group,** *see* management group

**marginal reserve requirement**
coefficient marginal de réserve
*encaje legal adicional*
Additional deposits that, by law, depository institutions (e.g., banks) must set aside in their vaults or with the central bank. In the U.S., this applies to additional reserve requirements on increased managed liabilities imposed by the Federal Reserve, in order to curtail the expansion of bank lending.

**margin buying [stock exchange]**
achat à découvert
*compra en descubierto*
System whereby the purchaser furnishes only a specified fraction of the total purchase price of securities bought, with

the broker furnishing the balance and charging interest on that amount.

**margin requirements [stock exchange]**
pourcentage de couverture; couverture de l'opération
*límites legales (de las compras en descubierto)*
Legal requirements regulating the amount of credit that may be extended under the *margin buying* (q.v.) system.

**markdown,** *see* discount

**marketable bond**
obligation négociable
*bono comerciable; bono negociable*
Bond quoted continuously by a dealer.

**market maker**
teneur de marché
*agiotista*
A bank or a broker that is prepared to make a two-way price (to buy or sell) for a currency or a security on a continuous basis, in the same way as a stock jobber in the U.K. market.

**market-related lending**
prêts aux conditions du marché
*financiamiento en condiciones de mercado*
Lending at market rate and under market conditions (cf. *commercial lending*).

**matched funding,** *see* back-to-back (4.)

**matched-maturity transaction [IBRD]**
opération à échéances symétriques
*transacción de vencimientos simultáneos*
A type of cross-currency interest hedge (q.v.), where the proceeds of a short-term instrument program are swapped for comparable maturities in other currencies.

**matched sale-purchase transaction**
transaction simultanée d'achat et de vente
*compra y venta simultánea*
Selling U.S. Treasury bills for cash and at the same time purchasing the same issue of bills for redelivery a day or more later.

**maturity arbitrage,** *see* time arbitrage

**merchant bank [U.K.],** *see* investment bank

**merry-go-round effect**
effet de carrousel
*efecto carrusel*
The circulation of money through various sources, ending up where it started. For instance the German Central Bank recycles excess capital by selling U.S. dollars to banks under a repurchase agreement and the banks place the U.S. dollars in the Euromarket. As the financial institutions could run up a U.S. dollar debt on the Euromarket, the Central Bank must buy back the U.S. dollars and sell domestic currency to avoid an excessive increase in the mark.

**mismatch risk [IBRD]**
risque lié au décalage entre les échéances
*riesgo relacionado con un desfase*
Risk of having loans and borrowings with mismatched maturities.

**money at call,** *see* call money

**money-center banks**
banques installées sur les principales places financières
*bancos establecidos en las principales plazas financieras*

**money market (mutual) fund; mutual fund**
fonds commun de placement
*fondo común de inversiones; fondo mutuo*

**mortgage bond**
titre hypothécaire; billet de mobilisation
*bono hipotecario; título hipotecario;cédula hipotecaria*

**multibank,** *see* combined commercial and investment bank

**multicurrency option**
option de change
*opción de cambio de divisa*
Procedure which allows a borrower to receive a loan in a currency other than the one specified, provided this currency is available on the market.

**multiple (currency) option bond**
obligation avec option de change; obligation avec option monétaire
*bono con opción de cambio de divisa*
Bond (usually Eurobond) which gives the lender the right to opt to receive interest and/or capital in a currency other than that in which the bond is denominated.

**multilateral netting**
compensation des créances internes
*compensación de débitos y créditos*
Procedure whereby a company with multinational trade flows is able to balance its debits and credits between subsidiaries and associates leaving only the balance to be settled, thereby reducing its need to acquire foreign currency.

**mutual fund,** *see* money market (mutual) fund

## - N -

**naked,** *see* uncovered

**name market**
marché où la cote de crédit est primordiale
*mercado basado en el prestigio de los prestatarios*
Market where great emphasis is placed on the standing and reputation of the borrowers (e.g., the Eurodollar market).

**narrow money [cf. M1]**
monnaie, masse monétaire au sens étroit
*dinero en el sentido estricto*

**near-bank [Canada]**
quasi-banque
*cuasibanco*
Financial institution, excluding standard commercial bank, such as a savings bank, credit union, etc.

**near-money; quasi-money**
quasi-monnaie
*cuasidinero*
Assets which have properties resembling those of money in the strict sense. Includes savings deposits, time deposits, certificates of deposits, deposits in thrift institutions, etc.

**negative-pledge clause**
clause de ne pas faire, négative, de nantissement négative
*cláusula de obligación negativa*
Clause in loan agreement obligating the borrower not to grant security without equally securing the loan in question.

**negotiable instrument**
effet de commerce
*instrumento negociable*
Instrument where the title passes on delivery or delivery and endorsement, where the current holder can sue in his own name, where no notice of assignment need be given to the person liable on the instrument, and where a holder in due course takes, free from any defect, in the title of his predecessors. Examples include bills of exchange, checks, and divided warrants.

**negotiable order-of-withdrawal (NOW) account**
compte-chèques rémunéré
*cuenta corriente que devenga intereses*
Interest-bearing checking account.

**negotiable time certificate of deposit**
certificat représentatif de dépôt à terme
*certificado de depósito negociable*
A deposit evidenced by a negotiable instrument, which provides on its face that the amount of the deposit is payable to the bearer or to his order on a certain date, after a certain specified time, upon notice in writing or upon presentation and surrender of the instrument, not less than thirty days after the date of the deposit.

**netting,** *see* multilateral netting

**net worth,** *see* stockholders' equity

**no-load fund**
fonds qui ne prélève pas une commission
*fondo de inversión que no cobra una comisión*
Money market fund that does not charge a fixed fee commission to investors.

**noncall period**
période d'interdiction de rachat
*período de prohibición de rescate*
Period during which a borrower may not give notice to redeem bonds, in Eurobond market.

**noncallable bond**
obligation ne pouvant être amortie par anticipation
*bono no rescatable, no redimible antes del vencimiento*

**nonmarketable bond**
obligation non négociable
*bono no comerciable; bono no negociable*

**nonmaturing, nonredeemable consol [U.K.]**
obligation perpétuelle; rente perpétuelle
*bono perpetuo*
government bond; perpetual bond;

**nonrecourse finance**
financement à forfait, sans recours
*financiamiento sin posibilidad de recurso*
A loan where the lenders look solely to the cash flow generated by the project being financed for repayment. There is no recourse to the sponsor of the project, so that the lenders assume all the commercial and political risks of the project.

**nonrecourse participation**
participation à forfait, sans recours
*participación sin posibilidad de recurso*

**nonredeemable government bond,** *see* nonmaturing bond

**note**
bon; obligation
*pagaré*
A bond with short- or medium-term maturity.

**NOW account,** *see* negotiable order of withdrawal

## - O -

**OBU,** *see* offshore banking unit

**offering memorandum**
mémorandum d'offre
*memorando de oferta*
Same as *prospectus* (q.v.)

**offshore bank**
banque off-shore
*banco extraterritorial*
Bank located outside the country in question.

**offshore banking center**
place bancaire off-shore; centre bancaire off-shore
*zona bancaria franca*
Financial center where many of the financial institutions have little connection with that country's financial system, usually for taxation purposes. Examples are the Cayman Islands where many of the corporations are engaged in business in the U.S. and Europe, and London where many of the financial institutions are engaged in Eurodollar trading.

**offshore banking unit (OBU)**
succursale off-shore
*departamento bancario considerado como extraterritorial*
Department within a bank that, in certain countries (e.g., Bahrain), is permitted to engage in specific transactions (usually Euromarket business) that ordinary domestic banks are not allowed to do.

**off-the-board market,** *see* third market

**onlending**
rétrocession
*représtamo*

**open-end (investment) fund; unit trust [U.K.]**
société d'investissement à capital variable (SICAV)
*sociedad de inversiones con número de acciones variable*
Investment company that has no fixed number of shares outstanding.

**open market**
1. open market; 2. marché financier
*1. mercado abierto; 2. mercado financiero*
1. The market maintained by government securities dealers. As regards U.S. Treasury borrowing operations, the open market is the money market in the case of short-term obligations or the capital market in the case of long-term obligations. 2. The general financial market.

**open pricing**
fixation libre des prix
*fijación de precios abierta*
Procedure whereby a bond issue is sold on the basis of a yield to be determined after the selling period is over.

**operating ratio**
coefficient net d'exploitation
*coeficiente de operación; coeficiente neto de explotación*
Ratio of operating costs (including depreciation) to total revenue.

**operating ratios**
ratios de gestion
*relaciones de gestión*
Ratios used to determine a corporation's operations; usually relate to sales, profits, and/or turnover.

**option**
option
*opción*
A contract giving the holder the right to buy or sell a stated number of shares (normally one hundred) of a particular security at a fixed price within a predetermined period. The Paris market has three main types of option : *prime, option*, and *stellage. Prime* is a call option. If the purchaser decides not to exercise his option (because the price has gone down), he merely has to pay the seller a fee, called a *dont*, the rate of which is fixed by the *Chambre syndicale des agents de change. Option* is more similar to the U.S. system and can be a put or call option. The purchaser pays a premium (*avec*) (q.v.), which is negotiated, whether he exercises the option or not. *Stellage* is the equivalent of the U.S. *straddle* (q.v.).

**original-issue discount bond**
obligation à prime d'émission
*bono emitido con descuento*
Bond with a rate of interest below that demanded by the market place and sold at a price at a significant discount to par.

**OTC**, *see* over-the-counter market

**out-of-(the)-money option**
option d'achat d'obligations à rendement réduit
*opción de compra de bonos con rendimiento inferior al del bono inicial*
Warrant option for bond at lower yields than original bond.

**outward swap**
report de devises
*reventa de divisas en moneda nacional*
Spot purchase of foreign exchange and forward resale of the same currency against domestic currency.

**overall risk profile [IBRD]**
profil des risques de financement
*perfil general del financiamiento*
Exposure profile of the World Bank. The difference between outgoings committed and amount needed to fund these outgoings. Also known as *the gap.*

**overhang**
offre excédentaire
*exceso de oferta*
Excess, normally of supply over demand (e.g., in the bond market).

**overnight funds**
argent au jour le jour
*fondos de un día para otro*

**over-the-counter market (OTC)**
marché hors cote
*mercado extrabursátil; mercado fuera de bolsa*
Market for securities not listed in any of the exchanges (about 80 percent of total securities in the U.S.). In the U.S., includes U.S. Government and agency issues, state and local government bonds, railroad bonds and shares, many public utility bonds and shares, and most corporation and bank shares.

**owners' equity**, *see* stockholders' equity

## - P -

**paid-up stock; fully paid stock**
actions libérées
*acciones pagadas*
Stock fully paid for (i.e., upon which no further subscription instalments are due).

**parallel financing**
financement parallèle
*financiamiento paralelo*
Cofinancing, but with the partners financing different parts of the project.

**parallel market**
marché parallèle
*mercado paralelo*
Market operating in "parallel" to the main money market (e.g., bank current and savings accounts) and including interbank loans and negotiable certificates of deposit.

**pari passu clause**
clause pari passu
*cláusula pari passu*
Clause in loan agreement precluding subordination of the loan to other debt. In the issue of new shares, it states that the new shares will rank equally for dividend with an existing similar issue.

**participating bond**, *see* income bond

**participation certificate**
1. bon de participation 2. *see* pass-through certificate
*certificado de participación*
Security incorporating the right to participate in the ownership of a corporation but without some of the rights granted to shareholders, such as the right to vote at shareholders' meetings.

**participation fee**
*commission de participation*
comisión de participación
A fee given to a bank participating in a Euroloan.

**partnership share**
part d'association
*participación en una sociedad*

**par value; face value**
valeur nominale
*valor nominal*
The principal or nominal value appearing on a bond, note, coupon, piece of money, or other instrument.

**pass-through certificate; participation certificate**
certificat de transfert de prêts
*certificado de transferencia de préstamos*
Issued by federal agencies, it represents undivided interest in pools of agency-owned assets (i.e., loans or mortgages). Initially offered with 30-year maturity, the interest and a portion of the principal are paid monthly.

**paying agent**
agent payeur
*agente pagador*
In the issue of international securities, firm (usually a bank) responsible for arranging for the payment of cash or checks to holders of the securities who will be receiving interest or dividends, etc.

**payment period** [IBRD]
tranche
*período de pago*
Interval between semiannual dates, on which repayment on IBRD loans is due.

**payout date**
date effective de rentrée des fonds; date de versement
*fecha de desembolso*

**payout price**
prix net; rentrée nette
*precio neto*
Difference between the face value of a bond and the net value received by the bondholder, after deducting commission.

**P/E ratio; PER,** *see* price/earnings ratio (P/E ratio; PER)

**perpetual bond,** *see* nonmaturing, nonredeemable government bond

**perpetual floating-rate note**
bon à intérêt variable perpétuel
*pagaré con tipo de interés flotante perpetuo*
A *floating-rate note* (q.v.) with interest paid on a three-monthly basis but which is renewable every six months (i.e., it has a floating maturity).

**personal stock,** *see* registered stock

**petrobond**
pétro-obligation
*petrobono*
Participation certificates which represent rights to a specific quantity of oil. Used primarily in Mexico.

**piggy-back financing**
financement gigogne
*financiamiento concatenado*

**placement memorandum; placing memorandum**
note d'information; mémorandum de placement
*memorando de información*
A document prepared by the lead manager of a syndicate in the Eurocredit market, which seeks to give sufficient information to other potential lenders to enable them to decide whether to participate in the credit.

**pool-based lending rate system** [IBRD]
système de taux prêteur fondé sur un pool d'emprunts
*sistema de tipos de interés basados en una "cesta" de empréstitos pendientes*

**pool-based variable lending rate** [IBRD]
taux prêteur variable basé sur un pool d'emprunts
*tipo de interés variable basado en una "cesta" de empréstitos pendientes*

**pooled loan**
prêt du pool
*préstamo incluido en el sistema de fondo común de monedas*
A loan included in the currency pooling system.

**post, to** (a rate)
fixer; annoncer (un taux)
*cotizar*

**praecipium; praecipuum**
préciput
*praecipuum; honorario del banco director*
The amount the lead manager of a Eurocredit takes for his own fee, before dividing the remainder of the management fee among the rest of the management group.

**preferred stock**
actions privilégiées; actions de priorité
*acciones preferenciales, preferentes, preferidas*
Stock which has a claim upon the earnings (and sometimes upon the assets and control) of a corporation prior to the common or other class stock.

**premier borrower,** *see* prime borrower

**premium** [foreign exchange]
report
*prima*
Opposite of *discount* (q.v.). A forward exchange rate standing at a premium over today's rate means that the currency concerned is more expensive in the forward market than now.

**premium** [option market]
avec
*prima*
Price at which an option sells. Cf. option.

**premium** [securities]
prime; agio
*prima; agio*
The difference between the par value and the higher market value of a security expressed as a percentage of the par value.

**premium** [stocks]
prime d'émission
*prima de emisión*
Difference between the face value and the selling price of the share when the selling price is higher.

**price** (of a bond)
cours; cotation
*precio*

**price/earnings ratio** (P/E ratio; PER)
coefficient de capitalisation des résultats (CCR); rapport cours-bénéfice
*relación precio-utilidades*
Market price per ordinary share divided by earnings per ordinary share after tax. It expresses the market value placed on the expectation of future earnings.

**primary dealer**
courtier (opérant sur le marché primaire)
*corredor (mercado primario)*

**primary market**
marché primaire
*mercado primario, de emisión*
Market for new security issues.

**prime borrower; premier borrower**
emprunteur bien coté, très solvable, de premier ordre
*prestatario preferencial, preferente, de primera clase*

**prime rate**
taux de base; taux privilégié
*tipo preferencial; tasa preferencial*
*Taux de base* is the rate charged by banks to preferential customers; *taux privilégié* is the rate charged by nonbank financial institutions (e.g., Crédit National).

**private paper**
effets privés
*efectos privados*
Paper placed with a limited group of investors and not advertised.

**private placement**
placement par voie privée
*colocación privada*

**profitability ratios; revenue-covenant ratios**
ratios de rentabilité
*relaciones de rentabilidad*
Ratios that measure the return on assets.

**project note**
bon à court terme émis (par une collectivité publique) pour financer un projet (autoamortissable)
*pagaré a corto plazo para financiar un proyecto*
Short-term paper issued by municipalities to finance short-term cash flows for a specific project.

**promissory note**
billet à ordre
*pagaré*
An unconditional promise in writing made by one person to another signed by the maker, engaging to pay, on demand or at a fixed or determinable future time, a sum of money to or to the order of a specified person, or to bearer.

**proprietary interest**
participation majoritaire dans l'actif; intérêt patrimonial; part de capital
*interés mayoritario*
An ownership interest, as in the interest held by an equity holder in a company or a patent holder who licenses use of the patent by others.

**prospectus**
prospectus; document
*prospecto*
A document containing all the pertinent information about a public offering of securities and about the borrower. It is made available to the appropriate legal authorities, stock exchanges, and the prospective investors by the lead manager. The French term *prospectus* is used in normal parlance; however, the term *document* is used in the legal instrument regulating the system (Ordinance No. 67-833 of September 28, 1967, Article 6). Also called *offering memorandum.*

**proxy borrowing** [IBRD]
élément du pool (provisoire) d'emprunts
*empréstitos de referencia*
IBRD borrowings between July 1, 1981 and June 3, 1982, which were used to calculate the lending rate for the first years of the pool-based variable lending rate.

**public offering** (of shares)
émission publique
*oferta pública; colocación pública*

**purchase and resale agreement** [Canada]
prise en pension des effets
*compromiso de compra y reventa*
Equivalent to the U.S. repurchase agreement (q.v.)

**purchased funds**
ressources acquises
*fondos comprados*
Include certificates of deposit, Eurodollar borrowings, federal funds, and repurchase agreements, as opposed to traditional bank liabilities (demand and time deposits).

**put option**
option de vente
*opción de venta*
A contract which entitles one party to it, at his option, to sell a specified amount of securities or commodities to the other party, at the price fixed in the contract, during the life of the contract.

**putable bond,** *see* retractable bond

## - Q -

**qualification stock**
actions de garantie
*acciones de garantía*

**qualified borrowings** [IBRD]
emprunts de référence
*empréstitos calificados*
Borrowings by IBRD after July 1, 1982 (i.e., based on the pool-based variable lending rate), using proxy borrowings (q.v.)

**quasi-money,** *see* near-money

**queue**
liste d'attente
*lista de espera*
The waiting list for the issue of securities (Switzerland, Federal Republic of Germany).

**quick ratio,** *see* acid-test ratio

## - R -

**RAN,** *see* revenue-anticipation note (RAN)

**rate, to; grade, to**
classer; coter
*clasificar, evaluar*

**rating agency**
agence de cotation, de classement (des titres)
*organismo de clasificación de valores*

**rational expectations**
anticipations rationnelles
*expectativas racionales*
A theory based, first, on the assumption that individuals and companies will try to maximize their own welfare—that is, they will try to make their own economic and other circumstances as desirable as possible—and, second, that, as individuals and companies make economic decisions in their own interest, they do so in such a way that markets move towards equilibrium, easing inflation.

**real interest rate**
taux d'intérêt réel
*tipo de interés real; tasa de interés real*
Normal rate less rate of inflation, divided by one plus the rate of inflation.

**red herring**
préavis d'émission
*anuncio preliminar de una nueva emisión*
Preliminary prospectus issued to obtain an indication of interest in the issue. It is incomplete because it does not contain the public offering price, the underwriter's discount, or the date of issue.

**red herring issue**
émission exploratoire
*emisión exploratoria*
An issue of bonds made on an experimental basis.

**rediscount**
réescompter
*redescontar*
Resale of instruments such as banker's acceptances already discounted by lender, usually with central bank or discount house, at a price less than the face value.

**refinancing risk [IBRD]**
risque de refinancement
*riesgo relacionado con el refinanciamiento*
Risk of not being able to refinance short-term borrowings under suitable conditions when these borrowings mature.

**registered stock; personal stock**
actions nominatives
*acciones nominativas*
Stock which cannot be transferred without placing the signature of the owner upon the books of the issuing corporation and delivery of the certificate.

**repos (RP),** *see* repurchase agreement

**repurchase agreement (RP; repos)**
contrat de report; mise en pension; accord de réméré
*acuerdo de recompra*
Arrangement by banks and other institutions to borrow short-term (usually one day) money by transferring securities to the lender, with the agreeement that they will buy them back.

**retained earnings**
report à nouveau; bénéfices non distribués
*utilidades no distribuidas*
Accumulated net income, less distributions to stockholders and transfers to paid-in capital accounts.

**retractable, putable bond**
obligation rétractable
*bono retractable*
Bond where coupon rate is determined for a limited number of years, after which a new coupon is determined, with bondholders at the same time having the right to early redemption.

**revaluation factor [currency pool]**
facteur de réévaluation
*factor de revaluación*
A ratio establishing the appreciation or depreciation due to exchange rate changes in the U.S. dollar value of currencies in the pool from one date to another. It is calculated by dividing, as of any day, the total U.S. dollar value at the exchange rates of that day of the balances of currencies in the pool brought forward from the previous day, by their total U.S. dollar value at the exchange rates of the previous day.

**revenue-anticipation note (RAN)**
obligation émise par une collectivité publique dans l'attente de rentrées non fiscales
*pagaré a corto plazo en espera de ingresos no tributarios*
Short-term municipal borrowings that fund current operations and are to be funded by revenues other than taxes, especially U.S. federal aid.

**revenue bond**
obligation à long terme émise par une collectivité publique pour financer un projet (dont les recettes assureront le remboursement)
*bono pagadero con los ingresos (del proyecto)*
Long-term borrowings that are used to fund specific projects. They are repaid from the income that will be generated by the project.

**revenue-covenant ratios,** *see* profitability ratios

**revolving credit**
crédit renouvelable, reconductible
*crédito rotatorio, renovable*

**revolving fund**
fonds renouvelable; caisse d'avances
*fondo rotatorio*
A fund for project-related expenditure.

**right (to purchase shares)**
droit
*derecho*
Usually issued in connection with new share issues. Gives the investor the right to purchase further shares at a given price.

**risk capital**
capital à risque
*capital de riesgo*
Capital invested in high-risk or relatively high-risk securities and enterprises, in expectation of commensurately high returns. It is sometimes used of equities or ordinary stock, the dividend of which varies with the profits earned by the corporation.

**risk premium**
prime de risque
*prima por riesgo*

**roll-over**
refinancement; reconduction; renouvellement
*refinanciamiento; renovación*

**roll-over certificate of deposit; roly-poly certificate of deposit**
certificat de dépôt à taux renouvelé renovable
*certificado de depósito con tipo de interés*
A package of certificates of deposit (CD) with maturity of, for example, three years, divided into six six-month periods. An investor buys the package as a whole but he may sell any of the six-month CDs on the secondary market. He is nevertheless committed to rolling over the CD by redepositing funds to the amount of the next six-month CD.

**roll-over credit**
crédit renouvelable, reconductible à taux variable
*crédito renovable, refinanciable*

**roll-over of gains**
réemploi des plus-values
*reutilización de las ganancias*

**roll-over risks**
risques de refinancement
*riesgos de refinanciamiento*

**roly-poly bond**
obligation à taux renouvelé
*bono con tipo de interés renovable*
Medium- or long-term bond whose annual coupon is renewed every three years, at which time the investor may be reimbursed.

**roly-poly certificate of deposit,** *see* roll-over certificate of deposit

**RP,** *see* repurchase agreement (RP; repos)

**running (weighted) average**
moyenne (pondérée) mobile
*promedio móvil (ponderado)*
The average rate of interest applied to an outstanding loan, based on the rates applied on all previous disbursements, weighted, where necessary, to allow for different levels of disbursement.

# - S -

**sales agent [securities]**
agent de placement
*agente vendedor; corredor*

**Samurai bond**
obligation samourai
*bono samurai*
Bond issued on the Japanese market in yen outside Japan.

**savings bond [France, Belgium, U.S.]**
bon de caisse; bon d'épargne
*bono de ahorro*
Short- or medium-term fixed-interest bearer bond issued by a public credit institution or commercial bank. Not marketable. *Bons de caisse* are general French savings bonds. *Bons d'épargne* are five-year savings bonds issued at par. The bearer can ask to be reimbursed after three months but the amount he is paid increases over the five-year period.

**scrip certificate; bearer scrip**
bulletin de livraison; certificat d'action partiellement libérée
*certificado provisional; título provisional*
Written obligation of a bank acting as paying agent for an issue, to hand over to the subscriber the definitive certificates as soon as they have been issued.

**secondary market**
marché secondaire
*mercado secundario*
Market for transactions in existing securities.

**secondary offering**
placement d'actions détenues par les particuliers
*colocación en el mercado secundario*
Redistribution of an outstanding block of stock by a securities firm. It is handled privately off the organized exchanges after the close of the market, at a fixed price not exceeding the last sale price on the floor.

**sector**, *see* segment

**securities analyst**
analyste des valeurs
*analista de valores*
Person carrying out systematic assessment of securities as a basis for investment strategy.

**securities dealer; securities firm**
courtier (en valeurs mobilières); maison de titres; société de placement
*corredor de valores; sociedad de valores*

**securities margin account**
compte d'achat de titres
*ganancia bruta en cuenta de valores*
Special account opened by private individuals for the purchase of securities, paid for partially by cash payments and partially on credit given by the broker up to a limit fixed by law.

**security**
titre; valeur mobilière
*valor; título*
1. Document giving title to property or claim on income. 2. Income-yielding paper traded on the stock exchange or secondary market.

**security lending [IBRD]**
prêts de titres
*préstamo en valores*
Lending of securities which the IBRD owns (typically a U.S. Government obligation) against receipt of cash or similar securities as collateral in amounts equal to or higher than the market value of the security lent.

**segment; sector (of the market)**
compartiment (du marché)
*segmento; sector*

**self-liquidating credit**
crédit autoamortissable
*crédito autoamortizable*
Credit reimbursed by the income from the operation for which it was lent.

**sell-down**
rétrocession
*venta de un crédito fuera del consorcio*
The transfer of a credit from a bank within a syndicate to a bank outside the syndicate.

**selling fee [Euromarket]**
commission de placement
*comisión de ventas*

**selling consortium, group, syndicate [Euromarket]**
groupe de placement
*consorcio (bancario); grupo de colocación; grupo vendedor*

**selling rate**
cours vendeur
*precio vendedor; precio de venta*
Price proposed (for a security).

**senior debt**
dette prioritaire
*deuda prioritaria*
Debt for which claims on the assets of the borrower rank ahead of other debts in case of liquidation.

**serial bond, loan**
1. emprunt par obligations émis par séries; 2. obligation à lot
*1. bono de vencimiento escalonado; 2. bono con vencimiento elegido a la suerte*
1. Bond issues split into a series of maturities. 2. Special type of serial bonds where reimbursement is decided by drawing in lots (used in France).

**shake-out (of the market)**
tassement
*1. asentamiento; 2. sacudimiento*
1. A moderate stock market or business recession, usually corrective of an inflationary condition. 2. Any movement in the market prices of securities that forces speculators to sell their holdings.

**shareholders' equity, funds**, *see* stockholders' equity

**share list**
cours de la Bourse
*lista de acciones con sus cotizaciones*
A listing of stocks with their current prices.

**shareownership**
avoirs en portefeuille; acquisition de valeurs mobilières, actions
*cartera de acciones*

**share-premium account [IFC]**
compte "prime d'émission"
*cuenta de primas de emisión*
Account of a corporation, in which IFC has a holding and in which the premiums obtained on new shares are deposited.

**share-retention agreement [IFC]**
accord de non-rétrocession d'actions
*acuerdo de retención de acciones*
Agreement, under which a company agrees not to sell the stock of another company in which IFC has an interest, until the loan has been reimbursed.

**shelf registration**
enregistrement en attente
*autorización permanente*
A system of standing authorization to issue securities given by the U.S. Treasury to certain select borrowers (including the IBRD). Borrowers must normally wait for formal approval.

**short hedge**
opération de couverture par vente à terme
*operación de cobertura por venta a plazo*
Hedging operation by someone who is "short" (i.e., who owns less of an item than he has contracts to deliver).

**short position**
engagement à la baisse
*posición de venta en descubierto*
Where a dealer in stocks or commodities is committed to sell more of them than he has available for sale.

**short sale**
vente à découvert
*venta en descubierto*
Sale by dealers of securities they do not own.

**short-term note**
effet à court terme
*pagaré a corto plazo*

**short-term paper**
effets à court terme; papier à court terme
*efectos a corto plazo; valores a corto plazo; papel a corto plazo*

**short-term paper market**
marché des effets à court terme
*mercado de corto plazo*

**sinking fund**
caisse d'amortissement; fonds d'amortissement
*fondo de amortización*
A fund created by a borrower for the purpose of redeeming bonds. The borrower is obliged to redeem specified amounts of the bond within specified periods.

**soundness certificate**
certificat de solvabilité (établi par une banque)
*certificado de solvencia*

**source and application of funds statement,** *see* statement of changes in financial position

**source and use of funds statement,** *see* statement of changes in financial position

**sovereign credit**
emprunt garanti par l'Etat
*crédito garantizado por el Estado*
A borrowing guaranteed by the state.

**sovereign risk**
risque d'insolvabilité de l'Etat emprunteur; risque souverain
*riesgo soberano; riesgo que plantea el país*
The risk of changes in a borrowing country's overall foreign exchange position, which might affect its ability to repay a loan.

**space arbitrage,** *see* two-point arbitrage

**special placement**
placement spécial
*colocación especial*
Placements issued by international development institutions and placed directly with central banks, monetary authorities, and governments.

**split; split-up**
division d'une action en plusieurs titres
*división de acciones*
Increasing the number of shares of a corporation by some ratio or multiple.

**spot market; cash market [foreign exchange]**
marché au comptant
*mercado al contado*

**spot market [commodities]**
marché du disponible
*mercado de productos disponibles, de entrega inmediata*

**spread**
1. 2. écart; 3. marge
*1. 2. 3. margen; diferencia; diferencial*
1. Options: Purchase of a call option at one price and resale at another. 2. Commodities: Purchase of a contract in one delivery month and resale in another. 3. Euromarket, securities: Difference between rate at which bank borrows money on interbank market and rate at which it onlends funds to its customers.

**spread risk [IBRD]**
risque lié à la marge
*riesgo relacionado con el margen*
Risk due to the spread between IBRD borrowing and loans being too low or negative.

**statement of changes in financial position; source and application of funds statement; funds statement; source and use of funds statement; flow statement; changes in working capital statement**
tableau de financement; tableau des flux
*estado de flujo de fondos*
A statement used in conventional accounting which summarizes the financing and investing activities of an entity, including the extent to which the enterprise has generated funds from operations during the period and for completing the disclosure of changes in financial position during the period. The first English term is the one recommended by the U.S. Accounting Principles Board (APB) since 1971; the second term is the one found most frequently in the World Bank and IFC; and the third is the most common one used in the U.S. prior to the APB recommendation. The other terms are also found.

**step-down (security)**
(titre à) coupon dégressif multiple
*valor con tipo de interés descendente*
Securities where the coupon rate decreases by a fixed amount every year.

**stepped-rate bond**
obligation à taux flottant fixé d'avance
*bono con tipos de interés escalonados (fijados anticipadamente)*
Bond with different coupon rates of interest for different periods, fixed in advance of the issue.

**stock dividend**
distribution d'actions gratuites; attribution d'actions gratuites
*dividendo en acciones*
A dividend paid to stockholders in share of stock of the issuing corporation.

**stockholders' equity; shareholders' equity; owners' equity; equity; net worth; shareholders' funds [U.K.]**
fonds propres; capitaux propres; situation nette
*patrimonio; patrimonio neto; activo neto*
The value of assets less liabilities of a corporation. All the terms given here are generally synonymous, but accountants tend to give different slants to these terms in certain cirumstances, so they may, on occasion, have slightly different meanings. For example, *capitaux propres* and *situation nette* are normally synonymous, though *capitaux propres* sometimes equals *situation nette* less retained earnings (*report à nouveau*).

**stock option**
option de souscription
*opción de compra de acciones*

**stop-out price**
prix d'arrêt
*precio mínimo en subasta a la baja*
Uniform auction price (i.e., lowest price at which bids are accepted) at a Dutch auction (q.v.).

**straddle; call-and-put option**
stellage
*opción de venta y compra*
Double option consisting of a put and a call with same striking price.

**straight bond**
obligation classique
*bono clásico; bono ordinario*
Bond with unquestioned right to repayment of principal at a specified future date, unquestioned right to fixed interest payments on stated dates, and no right to any additional interest, principal, or conversion privilege.

**straight, tap certificate of deposit**
certificat de dépôt classique, par lot
*certificado de depósito sin límite, de libre compra*
Standard certificate of deposit, without any restrictions on amount available.

**striking price; exercise price**
prix d'exercice
*precio fijado en contrato (para ejercitar una opción de compra)*
Price a particular share must reach before an option to purchase the shares can be exercised.

**subborrower**
emprunteur secondaire, final
*subprestatario*

**subloan**
prêt secondaire, subsidiaire
*subpréstamo*

**subordinated debt,** *see* junior debt

**subordinated loan**
prêt non privilégié
*préstamo subordinado*

**subscription right**
droit de souscription
*derecho de suscripción*
The same as *right* (q.v.)

**swap (transaction)**
swap; crédit croisé
*swap[ bancos centrales]; intercambio de monedas; crédito recíproco; pase financiero*
A spot purchase of foreign exchange with simultaneous forward sale or vice versa. *Pase financiero* is an Argentinian system, related to the swap system, whereby persons or institutions making capital investments are given an "exchange guarantee," which guarantees that the funds can be reexchanged at a predetermined exchange rate on a specific date.

**switch**
arbitrage
*arbitraje*
Sale of paper which is no longer considered to have long-term possibilities and investment of the proceeds in securities considered more worthwile.

**switch, availability clause**
clause de disponibilité
*cláusula de disponibilidad*
In a roll-over credit agreement, a clause which allows a lender to lend in a currency other than the one stipulated in the agreement, if the stipulated currency is not available.

**switching value**
valeur critique; valeur seuil
*valor crítico*
The value that reverses the ranking of two alternative projects. For example, Farm A will produce beef with high technology equipment and few workers, while Farm B will consist of a low-technology operation employing many farm workers. Up to a weight of 1.5 on income going to the poor, Farm A has a higher rate of return. However, if a weight greater than 1.5 is given, Farm B will have a higher rate of return. The switching value, therefore, is 1.5.

**syndicate**
consortium; syndicat financier
*consorcio (bancario, de financiamiento)*

**syndicate, to (a loan)**
consortialiser
*concertar un préstamo a través de un consorcio (bancario, de financiamiento)*

**syndicated loan**
prêt syndiqué; prêt consortial
*préstamo de un consorcio*

**syndication**
formation d'un syndicat financier, d'un consortium
*formación de un consorcio (bancario, de financiamiento)*

**system repurchase agreement**
contrat de report
*acuerdo de recompra*
Purchase by the Federal Reserve of securities for a short period of time with an agreement to resell them at a specified price.

## - T -

**take-and-pay contract**
contrat de paiement contre livraison
*contrato de compra garantizada*
A guarantee to buy an agreed amount of a product or service provided it is delivered.

**take in, to (bills)**
prendre (des effets) en pension
*redescontar con compromiso de reventa*
Rediscount operation with promise to transfer the credit title back to the original lender.

**take-or-pay contract**
contrat d'achat ferme; contrat de prise ferme
*contrato firme de compra (sin derecho de rescisión)*
An unconditional guarantee to buy an agreed amount of a product or service whether or not it is delivered.

**take out, to [IBRD]**
renoncer
*renunciar a una garantía*
Waiver by a colender of a guarantee given by the World Bank, as the guaranteed portion of a coloan progressively comes within the range of normal maturities.

**take-over bid**
offre publique d'achat (OPA)
*oferta pública de compra*

**take-over option [IBRD]**
option de reprise (des dernières échéances d'un prêt commercial)
*opción de financiamiento residual*
Contingent commitment by the IBRD to take over any residual financing of a loan as it reaches its ten-year maturity.

**TAN**, *see* tax-anticipation note

**tap certificate of deposit**, *see* straight certificate of deposit

**tap issue**
émission à guichets ouverts
*emisión continua*

**tap security**
titre émis à jet continu, à guichets ouverts
*valor en venta continua*
Security that is continuously available and may be obtained on demand by investors.

**tax-anticipation note (TAN)**
bon garanti par les recettes prévues
*pagaré respaldado por ingresos fiscales previstos*
Short-term borrowing issued to fill temporary financing needs. It is backed by anticipated tax receipts and any unencumbered revenue of the community.

**tax buoyancy**
élasticité globale du système fiscal par rapport au produit intérieur brut (PIB)
*elasticidad tributaria global*
Total elasticity of the tax system (built-in elasticity plus elasticity due to discretionary changes in the tax system). Measured by the annual mean growth in receipts divided by the annual mean growth in gross domestic product (GDP).

**tax credit**
avoir fiscal; crédit d'impôt
*descuento impositivo*

**term loan**
crédit d'équipement
*préstamo a mediano o largo plazo*
Medium- or long-term loan undertaken by a corporation when it cannot or does not want to issue a loan on the financial market.

**third market; off-the-board market**
troisième marché; marché hors bourse
*tercer mercado; mercado fuera de bolsa*
Market for security dealing in over-the-counter stocks listed on a stock exchange but between firms that are not members of an exchange and, therefore, do not charge regular listed commission.

**time arbitrage**
arbitrage dans le temps
*arbitraje en el tiempo*
Buying and selling at different maturities.

**tombstone**
avis financier; encart publicitaire
*anuncio de emisión efectuada; esquela*
Advertisement which announces that a credit has been arranged or a bond issue made.

**top-rated bond**
obligation de premier ordre
*bono de primer orden, de primera clase*

**trade bill [U.K.]**
effet de commerce
*letra comercial; efecto comercial*
Commercial bill accepted directly by a corporation.

**trading ticket [securities]**
fiche de Bourse; ordre d'achat; ordre de vente
*orden de compra; orden de venta*
Purchase/sales order for a security.

**tranche certificate of deposit**
certificat de dépôt par tranche
*certificado de depósito de tramo*
Certificate of deposit representing a share in a program of certificate-of-deposit issues by a bank.

**transfer price**
prix de transfert; prix interne; prix de cession interne
*precio de transferencia interna*
Price between a corporation and its subsidiary or within a corporation (opposite of *arm's length price*).

**transferable share**
action au porteur
*acción al portador; acción transferible; acción negociable*

**transformation**
transformation (bancaire)
*transformación (bancaria)*
Medium- and long-term reinvestment operations by financial intermediaries, taking in liquid savings or sight deposits.

**Treasury bill [U.S.]**
bon du Trésor en comptes courants
*pagaré del Tesoro a corto plazo*
Bill issued by U.S. Treasury with short maturity (less than one year).

**Treasury bond [U.S.]**
bon du Trésor à long terme
*bono del Tesoro*
Long-term (more than ten years) fixed coupon paper issued by the Federal Reserve on behalf of the U.S. Treasury.

**Treasury note [U.S.]**
bon du Trésor
*pagaré del Tesoro*
A medium-term (normally from two to ten years) coupon security issued by the U.S. Treasury. In France, *bons du Trésor* have a maturity of one to five years.

**Treasury tax and loan account [U.S.]**
compte courant du Trésor auprès des grandes banques
*cuenta corriente del Tesoro*
Current account of the U.S. Treasury in

which tax receipts and the receipts from the sale of bonds to the public are deposited.

**trigger clause [IBRD]**
clause de déclenchement
*cláusula de revisión*
Clause in IBRD loan agreement requiring review after a certain number of years to determine whether changes in the country's economic condition warrant harder or softer loans.

**trigger rate**
seuil de déclenchement
*tasa de activación*
Rate at which floating-rate notes are automatically converted to fixed-rate paper.

**trust bank (Shintaku Ginko) [Japan]**
banque de fiducie
*banco fiduciario*
Bank involved in both lending and money management.

**two-point arbitrage; space arbitrage**
arbitrage dans l'espace
*arbitraje espacial*
Buying in one center and selling in another.

## - U -

**uncovered; naked**
à découvert
*descubierto*
Unhedged (i.e., a liability exists in the long or short term, which is not covered by a corresponding position).

**underwriting consortium, group, syndicate**
1. groupe de garantie; syndicat de garantie; 2. syndicat de prise ferme
*1. grupo garante; grupo de suscripción; 2. consorcio de suscriptores*
1. Group that agrees with the issuer of securities to buy or find buyers for those securities that are not taken up by the public. 2. Group that buys up an entire issue of securities.

**underwriting fee**
commission de garantie
*comisión de suscripción; comisión de garantía*

**unit trust,** *see* open-end fund

**unlisted (security)**
non coté; non admis, non inscrit à la cote officielle
*no cotizado en la bolsa*
Security not listed for trading on one of the regular stock exchanges and which is, therefore, traded directly or over the counter.

**unrealized gains**
plus-values latentes
*ganancias no realizadas*

## - V -

**value date**
date de valeur
*fecha de valor*
The calendar date on which a transaction takes place.

**venture capital company**
société de financement de l'innovation
*compañía de capitales de riesgo*

## - W -

**warrant**
warrant
*certificado para la compra de acciones, bonos*
Option to purchase ordinary share or bond of a particular company, usually purchased by bondholder wanting to participate in profit growth of that company. Often attached to new bond issue as inducement for investors to take up the bond.

**warrant bond**
obligation à warrant; obligation warrantée
*bono con certificado*
Bond with warrant attached.

**warrant into government securities (WINGS)**
warrant échangeable contre des titres d'Etat
*certificado para la compra de pagarés del Tesoro*
Warrant which allows the purchaser to acquire, within a specified period of time, at a fixed price, a U.S. Treasury bill of specified coupon rate and maturity.

**wash sale**
transaction fictive
*transacción ficticia*
Occurs when a person buys and sells a stock, thereby recording a price, but with no actual change of ownership having taken place.

**weighted average,** *see* running average

**window (in a market)**
créneau
*resquicio*
Short-lived opportunity to issue securities that may be taken up by any of a significant number of highly rated borrowers.

**window dressing**
habillage du bilan
*manipulación de la contabilidad (para aparentar una mejor situación)*
Financial actions such as stock market trading, whose purpose is to make a corporation's financial situation seem better than it really it is, just before the publication of a balance sheet or other financial statement.

**WINGS,** *see* warrant into government securities

**working-capital ratio,** *see* current ratio

**working ratio**
coefficient brut d'exploitation
*coeficiente de explotación*
Cash working expenses divided by operating revenues, expressed as a percentage.

## - Y -

**Yankee bond**
obligation Yankee
*bono yanqui*
Bond issued on the U.S. market in U.S. dollars outside U.S.

**yield curve**
courbe des rendements
*curva de rendimiento*
Graph relating rates of return to maturity.

**yield to maturity (YTM)**
rendement à l'échéance
*rendimiento al vencimiento*

The return a security earns assuming that it is held until a certain date and put to the borrower at the specified put price.

**YTM,** *see* yield to maturity

## - Z -

**zero-coupon bond**
obligation à coupon zéro
*bono sin cupón*

Bond that pays no interest but is sold at a steep discount and paid off at par.

*Terminologie des emprunts et des prêts*

Français—Anglais

# - A -

**à découvert**
uncovered; naked

**acceptation de banque**
bank bill; banker's acceptance

**accord de compensation**
clearing agreement

**accord de non-rétrocession d'actions**
share-retention agreement [IFC]

**accord de paiement**
clearing agreement

**accord de réméré**
repurchase agreement (RP; repos)

**accord de swap sur les taux d'intérêt**
interest-rate swap

**achat à découvert**
margin buying [stock exchange]

**acquisition de valeurs mobilières, actions**
shareownership

**action au porteur**
transferable share

**action de jouissance**
dividend-right share

**action gratuite**
bonus share

**actions bénéficiaires**
dividend stock

**actions cumulatives privilégiées**
cumulative preferred stock

**actions de capital**
common stock

**actions de garantie**
qualification stock

**actions de priorité**
debenture stock [U.S.]

**actions de priorité**
preferred stock

**actions libérées**
paid-up stock; fully paid stock

**actions nominatives**
registered stock; personal stock

**actions ordinaires**
common stock

**actions privilégiées**
preferred stock

**adjudication à prix uniforme**
Dutch auction [U.S.]

**agence de cotation, de classement (des titres)**
rating agency

**agent**
agent bank

**agent boursier**
broker; dealer [stock market]

**agent boursier opérant pour son propre compte**
jobber

**agent de change**
broker [options market]

**agent de contrepartie**
dealer

**agent financier**
fiscal agent

**agent de placement**
sales agent [securities]

**agent opérant directement sur le parquet**
floor trader

**agent payeur**
paying agent

**agio**
agio; premium

**amélioration des prix moyens (d'un titre)**
averaging

**amortissement**
amortization

**analyste des valeurs**
securities analyst

**annoncer (un taux)**
post, to (a rate)

**anticipations rationnelles**
rational expectations

**approfondissement du capital**
capital deepening

**après bourse**
after-market

**arbitrage**
arbitrage; switch

**arbitrage dans l'espace**
two-point arbitrage; space arbitrage

**arbitrage dans le temps**
time arbitrage

**arbitragiste**
arbitrageur

**argent au jour le jour**
call money; day-to-day money; demand money; money at call; overnight funds

**assise financière**
capital base

**attraction**
crowding-in

**attribution**
allotment

**attribution d'actions gratuites**
stock dividend

**augmentation de l'importance des circuits financiers**
financial deepening

**aval**
aval

**avance de préémission**
bond-anticipation note (BAN)

**avances à vue**
call money; day-to-day money; demand money; money at call

**avances non garanties**
clean advances

**avec**
premium

**avis financier**
tombstone

**avoir fiscal**
tax credit

**avoirs en portefeuille**
shareownership

# - B -

**banque à charte**
chartered bank

**banque à charte fédérale**
federally chartered bank [U.S.]

**banque à tout faire, à vocation générale**
combined commercial and investment bank; multibank; all-purpose bank

**banque d'affaires**
investment bank [U.S.]; merchant bank [U.K.]

**banque de dépôt, commerciale**
commercial bank; clearing bank [U.K.]

**banque de fiducie**
trust bank (Shintaku Ginko) [Japan]

**banque "multiservices", à tout faire, à vocation générale, polyvalente**
combined commercial and investment bank; multibank; all-purpose bank

**banque off-shore**
offshore bank

**banque polyvalente**
combined commercial and investment bank; multibank; all-purpose bank

**banques installées sur les principales places financières**
money-center banks

**bénéfices non distribués**
retained earnings

**billet à ordre**
promissory note

**billet de mobilisation**
mortgage bond

**blanc**, *voir* (en) blanc

**bon**
note

**bon à court terme émis (par une collectivité publique) pour financer un projet (autoamortissable)**
project note

**bon à intérêt variable perpétuel**
perpetual floating-rate note

**bon à prime (d'émission)**
discount note

**bon à taux flottant**
floating-rate note [FRN]

**bon à taux révisable**
floating-rate note [FRN]

**bon au porteur**
bearer note

**bon de caisse**
savings bond [France, Belgium, U.S.]

**bon de jouissance**
dividend-right certificate

**bon d'épargne**
savings bond [France, Belgium, U.S.]

**bon de participation**
participation certificate

**bon du Trésor**
Treasury note [U.S.]

**bon du Trésor à long terme**
Treasury bond [U.S.]

**bon du Trésor à très court terme**
cash-management bill

**bon du Trésor en comptes courants**
Treasury bill [U.S.]

**bon garanti par les recettes prévues**
tax-anticipation note (TAN)

**bon-coupon**
coupon note

**bons à prime (d'émission) consolidés**
consolidated discount notes

**bulletin de livraison**
scrip certificate; bearer scrip

## - C -

**caisse d'amortissement**
sinking fund

**caisse d'avances**
revolving fund

**calendrier des émissions**
issuing calendar

**capacité d'endettement**
credit standing; creditworthiness

**capital à risque**
risk capital

**capital social**
equity capital; capital stock (of a corporation)

**capitalisation**
capitalization

**capitaux fébriles**
hot money; funk money

**capitaux propres**
stockholders' equity; shareholders' equity; owners' equity; equity; net worth; shareholders' funds [U.K.]

**centième de pour cent**
basis point

**centre bancaire off-shore**
offshore banking center

**certificat d'action partiellement libérée**
scrip certificate; bearer scrip

**certificat de dépôt**
certificate of deposit (CD)

**certificat de dépôt à taux renouvelé**
roll-over certificate of deposit; roly-poly certificate of deposit

**certificat de dépôt classique, par lot**
straight, tap certificate of deposit

**certificat de dépôt d'un montant minimum de $100.000**
jumbo certificate of deposit

**certificat de dépôt par tranche**
tranche certificate of deposit

**certificat de reconnaissance de dette**
debt certificate

**certificat de solvabilité (établi par une banque)**
soundness certificate

**certificat de transfert de prêts**
pass-through certificate; participation certificate

**certificat nominatif**
bond certificate

**certificat représentatif de dépôt à terme**
negotiable time certificate of deposit

**chambre de compensation**
clearing house

**chef de file**
lead bank; lead manager

**chèque banque**
banker's draft

**chèque tiré**
banker's draft

**classer**
rate, to; grade, to

**clause "drop lock"**
drop lock

**clause d'exigibilité croisée**
cross-default clause

**clause de déclenchement**
trigger clause [IBRD]

**clause de disponibilité**
switch, availability clause

**clause de manquement réciproque**
cross-default clause

**clause de ne pas faire, négative, de nantissement négative**
negative-pledge clause

**clause de sauvegarde**
jeopardy clause; disaster clause; break clause

**clause de verrouillage au taux plancher**
drop lock

**clause pari passu**
pari passu clause

**co-chef de file**
comanager; colead manager

**coefficient brut d'exploitation**
working ratio

**coefficient d'utilisation des fonds propres**
gearing ratio [IBRD]

**coefficient de Bruno**
Bruno ratio

**coefficient de capitalisation des résultats (CCR)**
price/earnings ratio (P/E ratio; PER)

**coefficient de coût en ressources intérieures**
domestic resource cost ratio

**coefficient marginal de réserve**
marginal reserve requirement

**coefficient net d'exploitation**
operating ratio

**coefficients de liquidité**
liquidity ratios

**commission de direction**
management fee

**commission de garantie**
guarantee commission, fee [IBRD]; underwriting fee

**commission de gestion**
agency fee [Euromarket]; management fee

**commission d'engagement**
commitment fee; stand-by fee

**commission de participation**
participation fee

**commission de placement**
selling fee [Euromarket]

**commission de reconduction**
extension fee

**commission d'ouverture**
front-end fee

**commission syndicale**
management fee

**compartiment (du marché)**
segment; sector (of the market)

**compensation des créances internes**
multilateral netting

**compte-chèques rémunéré**
negotiable order-of-withdrawal (NOW) account

**compte courant du Trésor auprès des grandes banques**
Treasury tax and loan account [U.S.]

**compte d'achat de titres**
securities margin account

**compte d'avances de caisse**
imprest account, fund

**compte d'avances temporaires**
imprest account, fund

**compte de gestion de trésorerie**
cash-management account

**compte de réserves pour le rachat du capital des actions**
capital redemption reserve funds

**compte "prime d'émission"**
share-premium account [IFC]

**concentration (des échéances)**
bunching (of maturities)

**consortialiser**
syndicate, to (a loan)

**consortium**
syndicate

**contrat d'achat ferme**
take-or-pay contract

**contrat de paiement contre livraison**
take-and-pay contract

**contrat de prise ferme**
take-or-pay contract

**contrat de report**
repurchase agreement (PR; repos); system repurchase agreement

**conversion monétaire**
currency translation

**correspondant**
agent bank

**cotation**
price (of a bond)

**cotation (de la barre d'or)**
fixing

**coter**
rate, to; grade, to

**coupon**
coupon

**courbe des rendements**
yield curve

**cours**
price (of a bond)

**cours acheteur**
bid price

**cours de la Bourse**
share list

**cours de l'offre**
ask(ed) price [securities market]

**cours vendeur**
selling rate

**courtage**
brokerage

**courtier**
broker

**courtier (en valeurs mobilières)**
securities dealer; securities firm

**courtier (opérant sur le marché primaire)**
primary dealer

**courtier d'effets publics**
government-security dealer

**courtier en fonds d'Etat**
government-security dealer

**courtier en placements**
investment broker

**coût des emprunts doublement pondéré**
double-weighted borrowing cost [IBRD]

**coût en ressources intérieures**
domestic resource cost (DRC)

**coût réel des devises**
domestic resource cost (DRC)

**couverture de l'opération**
margin requirements [stock exchange]

**couverture des opérations à terme**
hedging

**couverture du service de la dette**
debt-service coverage

**crédit à vue, à très court terme**
call money; day-to-day money; demand money; money at call

**(crédit) adossé**
back-to-back (loan, borrowing)

**crédit autoamortissable**
self-liquidating credit

**crédit consortial (sans chef de file)**
club loan

**crédit croisé**
swap (transaction)

**crédit d'équipement**
term loan

**crédit d'impôt**
tax credit

**(crédit) face à face**
back-to-back (loan, borrowing)

**crédit renouvelable, reconductible**
revolving credit

**crédit renouvelable, reconductible à taux variable**
roll-over credit

**créneau**
window (in a market)

**"cushion bond"**
cushion bond

## - D -

**date de valeur**
value date

**date de versement**
payout date

**date effective de rentrée des fonds**
payout date

**décote**
discount from par [securities market]

**décote de conversion**
conversion discount

**découvert,** *voir* à découvert

**dépenses groupées au début (d'une période donnée)**
front-loaded spending

**déport**
backwardation; disagio; discount; markdown [foreign exchange]

**désintermédiation**
disintermediation

**dette consolidée**
funded debt

**dette de deuxième rang**
junior debt; subordinated debt

**dette prioritaire**
senior debt

**disagio**
disagio

**distribution d'actions gratuites**
stock dividend

**division d'une action en plusieurs titres**
split; split-up

**document**
prospectus

**droit**
right (to purchase shares)

**droit de souscription**
subscription right

## - E -

**écart**
spread

**échange de monnaies différentes**
back-to-back (loan, borrowing)

**effet à court terme**
short-term note

**effet brûlant**
hot bill

**effet de carrousel**
merry-go-round effect

**effet de commerce**
negotiable instrument; trade bill [U.K.]

**effets à court terme**
short-term paper

**effets de commerce**
commercial paper; commercial bills

**effets de commerce en eurodevises**
Eurocommercial paper

**effets porteurs d'intérêt**
interest-bearing notes

**effets privés**
private paper

**effets publics**
government paper

**élargissement du capital**
capital widening

**élasticité globale du système fiscal par rapport au produit intérieur brut (PIB)**
tax buoyancy

**élément du pool (provisoire) d'emprunts**
proxy borrowing [IBRD]

**émetteur**
issuer; maker (e.g., of a note)

**émission à guichets ouverts**
tap issue

**émission collée**
hung-up issue

**émission d'obligations à l'étranger**
external bond issue

**émission de titres**
capital issue

**émission exploratoire**
red herring issue

**émission publique**
public offering (of shares)

**emprunt de contrepartie**
back-to-back (loan, borrowing)

**emprunt garanti par l'Etat**
sovereign credit

**emprunt global**
lump-sum borrowing [IFC]

**emprunt par obligations émis par séries**
serial bond, loan

**emprunt remboursable en une seule fois**
bullet issue

**emprunt remboursable *in fine***
bullet issue

**emprunteur bien coté, très solvable, de premier ordre**
prime borrower; premier borrower

**emprunteur secondaire, final**
subborrower

**emprunts de collectivité locale**
general obligations; general-obligation bonds

**emprunts de référence**
qualified borrowings [IBRD]

**emprunts géants**
jumbo borrowing

**(en) blanc**
clean

**encart publicitaire**
tombstone

**engagement**
exposure

**engagement à la baisse**
short position

**engagement conditionnel**
contingent obligation [IBRD]

**engagement par pays**
country exposure

**enregistrement en attente**
shelf registration

**érosion fiscale des revenus**
fiscal drag

**escompte**
discount [bills]

**escompte à forfait, en ducroire, sans recours**
discount without recourse

**escompte officiel**
discount window

**eurocrédit**
Eurocredit

**eurodevises**
Eurocurrency

**eurodollar**
Eurodollar

**euromarché**
Euromarket

**euromonnaie**
Eurocurrency

**euro-obligation**
Eurobond

**europrêt**
Euroloan

**évaluation actuarielle**
actuarial evaluation

**éviction**
crowding-out

## - F -

**facteur d'ajustement de l'amortissement**
amortization adjustment factor [currency pool]

**facteur de réévaluation**
revaluation factor [currency pool]

**fiche de Bourse**
trading ticket [securities]

**financement à forfait, sans recours**
nonrecourse finance

**financement avec droit de recours limité**
limited-recourse finance

**financement conjoint**
joint financing

**financement des dernières échéances**
funding latter maturities [IBRD]

**financement gigogne**
piggy-back financing

**financement parallèle**
parallel financing

**financement sur contrat**
contract financing

**fixation libre des prix**
open pricing

**fixer**
post, to (a rate)

**fixing**
fixing

**flottement impur, contrôlé, dirigé, assisté, soutenu**
dirty float

**flottement pur, non dirigé**
clean float

**fluctuation des taux due à une fuite de capitaux**
interest leakage

**flux financiers**
funds flow; flow of funds

**fonds commun de placement**
money-market (mutual) fund; mutual fund

**fonds d'amortissement**
sinking fund

**fonds de placement fermé**
closed-end (investment) fund

**fonds d'Etat britanniques**
gilt-edged securities

**fonds fédéraux**
federal funds

**fonds propres**
stockholders' equity; shareholders' equity; owners' equity; equity; net worth; shareholders' funds [U.K.]; capital base

**fonds qui ne prélève pas une commission**
no-load fund

**fonds qui prélève une commission**
load fund

**fonds renouvelable**
revolving fund

**forfaitage**
forfeiting

**formation d'un syndicat financier, d'un consortium**
syndication

**formules nouvelles, inédites, originales de financement**
creative financing

**frais de gestion**
management fee

**freinage fiscal**
fiscal drag

## - G -

**garantie (de l'Etat)**
guarantee

**garantie de la BIRD**
guarantee [IBRD]

**Gensaki**
Gensaki

**gestion de (la) trésorerie**
cash management

**gestion du passif**
liability management

**grande banque**
city bank

**groupe de direction**
management, managing group [Eurodollar market]

**groupe de garantie**
underwriting consortium, group, syndicate

**groupe de placement**
selling consortium, group, syndicate [Euromarket]

**guichet automatique de banque (GAB)**
automatic teller machine (ATM)

## - H -

**habillage du bilan**
window dressing

**honorabilité**
credit standing; creditworthiness

## - I -

**inflation de base**
core inflation

**instruments**
instruments

**instruments de la dette publique**
government debt instruments

**instruments financiers à terme**
financial futures

**intérêt de déport**
backwardation rate

**intérêt de report**
contango rate; continuation rate

**intérêt patrimonial**
proprietary interest

**intermédiaire financier**
financial intermediary

**intermédiation**
intermediation

**investissement de productivité**
capital-deepening investment

## - J -

**"jobber"**
jobber

## - L -

**lettre de change**
bill of exchange

**lettre de confort**
letter of comfort

**LIBOR**
LIBOR (London Interbank Offered Rate)

**ligne de crédit de protection, de soutien, auxiliaire**
back-up line of credit

**liste d'attente**
queue

## - M -

**M1**
M1

**M2**
M2

**M3**
M3

**maison d'acceptation**
acceptance, accepting house

**maison de réescompte**
discount house; bill broker

**maison de titres**
securities dealer; securities firm

**mandataire**
agent bank

**marché à terme**
forward market

**marché au comptant**
spot market; cash market

**marché de capitaux**
capital market

**marché de porteurs**
bearer market

**marché des effets à court terme**
short-term paper market

**marché du disponible**
spot market [commodities]

**marché figé**
locked market

**marché financier**
capital market; open market

**marché gris**
grey, gray market

**marché hors bourse**
third market; off-the-board market

**marché hors cote**
over-the-counter market (OTC)

**marché où la cote de crédit est primordiale**
name market

**marché parallèle**
parallel market

**marché primaire**
primary market

**marché secondaire**
secondary market

**marge**
spread

**masse monétaire au sens étroit**
narrow money

**masse monétaire au sens large**
broad money

**mémorandum de placement**
placement memorandum; placing memorandum

**mémorandum d'offre**
offering memorandum

**mise en pension**
repurchase agreement (RP; repos)

**mise en report**
inward swap

**mobiliser**
discount

**monnaie scripturale**
bank money

**monnaie au sens étroit**
narrow money

**monnaie au sens large**
broad money

**moyenne (pondérée) mobile**
running (weighted) average

**moyens de paiement à l'encaissement**
float [banking]

**moyens de paiement non recouvrés**
float [banking]

## - N -

**niveau d'indifférence**
break-even point [stock market]

**non admis, non inscrit à la cote officielle**
unlisted (security)

**non coté**
unlisted (security)

**non garanti**
clean

**note d'information**
placement memorandum; placing memorandum

## - O -

**obligation**
bond; debenture (bond); note

**obligation à coupon zéro**
zero-coupon bond

**obligation à long terme émise par une collectivité publique pour financer un projet**
revenue bond

**obligation à lot**
serial bond, loan

**obligation à prime (d'émission)**
discount bond

**obligation à prime d'émission**
original issue discount bond

**obligation à prime d'émission élevée**
deep-discount bond, note

**obligation à taux flottant**
floating-rate bond

**obligation à taux flottant fixé d'avance**
stepped-rate bond

**obligation à taux renouvelé**
roly-poly bond

**obligation à taux variable (OTV)**
floating-rate bond

**obligation à warrant**
warrant bond

**obligation assortie d'une option d'achat au-dessous du pair**
accreted call bond

**obligation au porteur**
bearer bond

**obligation avec option de change**
multiple (currency) option bond

**obligation avec option monétaire**
multiple (currency) option bond

**obligation "bouledogue"**
Bulldog bond

**obligation cautionnée**
custom-duty bill

**obligation classique**
straight bond

**obligation (cotée) AAA (marché américain)**
AAA bond

**obligation de premier ordre**
AAA bond; top-rated bond

**obligation de société**
corporate bond

**obligation émise par une collectivité publique dans l'attente de rentrées non fiscales**
revenue-anticipation note (RAN)

**obligation étrangère émise à Londres**
Bulldog bond

**obligation indexée**
indexed bond; index-linked bond

**obligation munie de coupon**
coupon(-bearing) bond

**obligation ne pouvant être amortie par anticipation**
noncallable bond

**obligation négociable**
marketable bond

**obligation non garantie**
debenture (bond)

**obligation non négociable**
nonmarketable bond

**obligation participante**
income bond; participating bond

**obligation perpétuelle**
nonmaturing, nonredeemable government bond; perpetual bond; consol [U.K.]

**obligation pouvant intéresser les banques**
bank quality bond

**obligation reconductible**
extendible note; extendible-maturity note

**obligation remboursable avant l'échéance**
callable bond

**obligation rétractable**
retractable, putable bond

**obligation samourai**
Samurai bond

**obligation vendue à guichet ouvert**
bond sold on tap

**obligation warrantée**
warrant bond

**obligation Yankee**
Yankee bond

**obligations émises par des organismes fédéraux**
agency securities, obligations

**offre excédentaire**
overhang

**offre publique d'achat (OPA)**
take-over bid

**open market**
open market

**opérateur (sur le marché)**
dealer [stock market]

**opération à échéances symétriques**
matched-maturity transaction [IBRD]

**opération couplée d'emprunts**
back-to-back (loan, borrowing)

**opération de couverture par vente à terme**
short hedge

**opérations à terme**
futures [commodities market]

**opérations d'arbitrage en couverture**
hedging

**opérations de couverture par achat à terme**
long hedge

**opérations en contrepartie**
hedging

**option**
option

**option d'achat d'obligations à rendement réduit**
out-of-(the)-money option

**option d'achat, de rachat**
call option

**option de change**
multicurrency option

**option de reprise (des dernières échéances d'un prêt commercial)**
take-over option)

**option de souscription**
stock option

**option de vente**
put option

**ordre d'achat**
trading ticket [securities]

**ordre de vente**
trading ticket [securities]

**organisme d'émission**
issuer

## - P -

**papier à court terme**
short-term paper

**papier commercial**
commercial paper; commercial bills

**papier financier**
commercial paper; commercial bills

**papiers**
instruments

**parité de conversion**
conversion value

**part bénéficiaire**
founder's share

**part d'association**
partnership share

**part de capital**
proprietary interest

**part de fondateur**
founder's share

**part des risques**
exposure

**part sociale**
corporate right

**participation à forfait, sans recours**
nonrecourse participation

**participation au capital social d'une société**
equity ownership

**participation majoritaire dans l'actif**
proprietary interest

**participation proportionnelle**
funding pro rata [IBRD]

**période d'interdiction de rachat**
noncall period

**pétro-obligation**
petrobond

**place bancaire off-shore**
offshore banking center

**placement d'actions détenues par les particuliers**
secondary offering

**placement de père de famille**
blue chip

**placement par voie privée**
private placement

**placement spécial**
special placement

**plus-values latentes**
unrealized gains

**point de base**
basis point

**pool de monnaies**
currency pool

**portefeuille de prêts**
loan portfolio

**portefeuille liquide**
liquidity portfolio

**porteur de titres, d'obligations**
bondholder

**pourcentage de couverture**
margin requirements [stock exchange]

**pouvoir d'engagement**
commitment authority

**préavis d'émission**
red herring

**préciput**
praecipium; praecipuum

**prendre (des effets) en pension**
take in, to (bills)

**prêt "A"**
"A" loan

**prêt au jour le jour**
call loan

**prêt "B"**
"B" loan

**prêt ballon**
balloon loan

**prêt cofinancé**
coloan

**prêt consortial**
syndicated loan

**prêt de titres garanti par d'autres titres**
borrow-pledge security loan

**prêt de titres garanti par des fonds**
cash security loan

**prêt du pool**
pooled loan

**prêt en cascade**
apex loan

**prêt en difficulté**
distressed loan

**prêt indexé**
indexed loan [currency pool]

**prêt non privilégié**
subordinated loan

**prêt pyramidal**
apex loan

**prêt secondaire, subsidiaire**
subloan

**prêt syndiqué**
syndicated loan

**prêteur de dernier recours**
lender of last resort

**prêteur en dernier ressort**
lender of last resort

**prêts aux conditions du marché**
market-related lending

**prêts de titres**
security lending [IBRD]

**prime**
premium

**prime de conversion**
conversion premium

**prime de liquidité**
liquidity premium

**prime d'émission**
discount [bonds]; premium

**prime de remboursement**
call premium

**prime de risque**
risk premium

**prime de risque-inflation**
inflation premium

**prise en pension**
buy-back [Canada]

**prise en pension des effets**
purchase and resale agreement [Canada]

**prise ferme**
bought deal

**prix acheteur**
buying rate [securities market]

**prix comptable**
accounting price

**prix d'arrêt**
stop-out price

**prix de cession interne**
transfer price

**prix de conversion**
conversion price

**(prix) de pleine concurrence**
arm's length (price)

**prix de transfert**
transfer price

**prix d'exercice**
striking price; exercise price

**prix économique**
economic price; efficiency price

**prix franco frontière**
border price

**prix frontière**
border price

**prix interne**
transfer price

**prix net**
payout price

**(prix) normal du marché**
arm's length (price)

**profil des risques de financement**
overall risk profile [IBRD]

**prospectus**
prospectus

**protection contre un rachat anticipé**
call protection

## - Q -

**quasi-banque**
near-bank

**quasi-monnaie**
near-money; quasi-money

**quatrième marché**
fourth market

## - R -

**rapport cours-bénéfice**
price/earnings ratio (P/E ratio; PER)

**rapport encours des prêts/fonds propres**
gearing ratio [IBRD]

**ratio de couverture de l'intérêt**
interest-coverage ratio

**ratio de levier**
leverage (ratio) [U.S.]; gearing (ratio) [U.K.]

**ratio de liquidité générale**
current ratio; working-capital ratio

**ratio d'endettement**
debt-equity ratio; debt-to-equity ratio

**ratio d'endettement à long terme**
long-term debt ratio

**ratio de solvabilité**
debt ratio

**ratio de solvabilité-endettement**
leverage (ratio) [U.S.]; gearing (ratio) [U.K.]

**ratio de structure du passif**
leverage (ratio) [U.S.]; gearing (ratio) [U.K.]

**ratio de trésorerie réduite**
acid-test, liquid, quick ratio

**ratio du service de la dette**
debt-service ratio

**ratio prix comptable–prix du marché**
accounting ratio

**ratio tiré du bilan**
balance-sheet ratio

**ratios de gestion**
operating ratios

**ratios de liquidité**
liquidity ratios

**ratios de rentabilité**
profitability ratios; revenue-covenant ratios

**ratios de structure**
financial ratios

**ratios financiers**
financial ratios

**reconduction**
roll-over

**réemploi des plus-values**
roll-over of gains

**réescompter**
rediscount

**refinancement**
roll-over

**refinancement anticipé**
advanced refunding

**refinancement pour un montant égal**
even roll

**réglage de précision**
fine-tuning (of the economy)

**remboursement [prêts]**
amortization

**remboursement en tranches égales**
level repayment

**remise (d'une dette)**
cancellation (of a debt)

**rendement à l'échéance**
yield to maturity (YTM)

**rendement converti en taux d'intérêt**
coupon-equivalent yield

**renoncer**
take out, to [IBRD]

**renouvellement**
roll-over

**rente perpétuelle**
nonmaturing, nonredeemable government bond; perpetual bond; consol [U.K.]

**rentrée nette**
payout price

**répartition**
allotment

**report**
contango; premium [foreign exchange]

**report à nouveau**
retained earnings

**report de crédits**
carry-over

**report de devises**
outward swap

**répression financière**
financial repression

**ressources acquises**
purchased funds

**rétrocession**
onlending; sell-down

**risque**
exposure

**risque de perte sur les taux d'intérêt**
interest-rate risk

**risque de refinancement**
refinancing risk [IBRD]

**risque d'insolvabilité de l'Etat emprunteur**
sovereign risk

**risque dû au décalage**
lag risk [IBRD]

**risque lié à la marge**
spread risk [IBRD]

**risque lié à la rentabilité des liquidités**
cash risk; liquid-holdings risk

**risque lié au décalage entre les échéances**
mismatch risk [IBRD]

**risque souverain**
sovereign risk

**risques de refinancement**
roll-over risks

## - S -

**sécurité**
comfort

**service bancaire international**
international banking facility (IBF)

**services bancaires de gestion financière**
bank trust departments

**seuil de déclenchement**
trigger rate

**simple**
clean

**situation nette**
stockholders' equity; shareholders' equity; owners' equity; equity; net worth; shareholders' funds [U.K.]

**société de financement de l'innovation**
venture capital company

**société de placement**
securities dealer; securities firm

**société de placement collectif**
investment company, fund

**société d'investissement**
investment company, fund

**société d'investissement à capital fixe**
closed-end (investment) fund

**société d'investissement à capital variable (SICAV)**
open-end (investment) fund; unit trust [U.K.]

**société d'investissement fermée**
closed-end (investment) fund

**société mandatée (par la Banque mondiale pour la représenter à des émissions d'obligations au Japon)**
commissioned company [Japan]

**solvabilité**
credit standing; creditworthiness

**sous-compte débiteur de l'emprunteur**
borrower's indebtedness subaccount [currency pool]

**stellage**
straddle; call-and-put option

**succursale off-shore**
offshore banking unit (OBU)

**surface financière**
credit standing; creditworthiness

**swap**
swap (transaction)

**swap de monnaies, sur le cours de change**
currency swap

**swap de taux d'intérêt**
interest-rate swap

**swap d'obligations à valeur nominale égale**
even par swap

**swap sur des dettes**
debt-for-debt swap

**swaps portant à la fois sur les taux d'intérêt et sur des monnaies**
cross-currency interest hedge; doublehedge swap

**syndicat de direction**
management, managing group [Eurodollar market]

**syndicat de garantie**
underwriting consortium, group, syndicate

**syndicat de prise ferme**
underwriting consortium, group, syndicate

**syndicat financier**
syndicate

**système fédéral de réserve**
Federal Reserve System [U.S.]

**système de taux prêteur fondé sur un pool d'emprunts**
pool-based lending rate system [IBRD]

**système du pool de monnaies**
currency pooling system

## - T -

**tableau de financement; tableau des flux**
statement of changes in financial position; source and application of funds statement; funds statement; source and use of funds statement; funds flow statement; changes in working capital statement

**tableau d'opérations financières**
flow-of-fund table [national accounts]

**tassement**
shake-out (of the market)

**taux critique de rentabilité**
hurdle rate

**taux d'activité**
activity ratios

**taux d'actualisation**
discount rate

**taux d'actualisation de la consommation**
consumption rate of interest (CRI)

**taux d'avances sur titres**
broker loan rate

**taux de base**
prime rate

**taux de change minimum**
floor rate of exchange

**taux de coupon**
coupon rate

**taux de coupon courant**
current coupon (rate)

**taux d'égalisation des valeurs actuelles**
cross-over discount rate; equalizing discount rate

**taux de l'argent au jour le jour**
call-money rate

**taux des avances à vue**
call-money rate

**taux des avances sur titres**
Lombard rate [Federal Republic of Germany]

**taux d'escompte**
discount rate

**taux des fonds fédéraux**
federal funds rate

**taux d'indifférence**
cross-over discount rate; equalizing discount rate

**taux d'intérêt comptable (TIC)**
accounting rate of interest (ARI)

**taux d'intérêt réel**
real interest rate

**taux Lombard**
Lombard rate

**taux plancher de verrouillage**
lock rate

**taux prêteur variable basé sur un pool d'emprunts**
pool-based variable lending rate [IBRD]

**taux privilégié**
prime rate

**tel quel**
flat

**teneur de marché**
market maker

**teneur de plume**
lead bank; lead manager

**titre**
security

**(titre à) coupon dégressif multiple**
step-down (security)

**titre au porteur**
bearer security

**titre de rente**
annuity bond

**titre émis à jet continu, à guichets ouverts**
tap security

**titre en dépôt**
depositary receipt

**titre hypothécaire**
mortgage bond

**titre précurseur**
bellwether security

**titre relevé**
book-entry security

**titres assortis de coupons**
coupon paper

**titres de placement**
investment securities

**traduction monétaire**
currency translation

**traite à un certain délai de vue**
after-sight bill

**tranche**
payment period [IBRD]

**transaction fictive**
wash sale

**transaction simultanée d'achat et de vente**
matched sale-purchase transaction

**transactions d'initiés**
inside, insider dealing

**transfert de fonds électronique**
electronic funds transfer (EFT)

**transformation (bancaire)**
transformation

**troisième marché**
third market; off-the-board market

## - U -

**unité européenne de compte (uec)**
European Unit of Account (EUA)

**unité monétaire européenne (écu)**
European Currency Unit (ECU)

## - V -

**valeur comptable**
book value

**valeur cotée en Bourse**
listed security

**valeur critique**
switching value

**valeur de père de famille**
blue chip

**valeur de premier ordre**
blue chip

**valeur de refuge**
hedge

**valeur mobilière**
security

**valeur nominale**
par value; face value

**valeur nominale totale**
full face value

**valeur seuil**
switching value

**valeurs garanties par l'Etat**
gilt-edged securities

**valeurs de premier ordre**
gilt-edged securities

**vente à découvert**
short sale

**vente sans garantie d'émission**
best-efforts sale

## - W -

**warrant**
warrant

**warrant détachable**
detachable warrant

**warrant échangeable contre des titres d'Etat**
warrant into government securities (WINGS)

**warrant en devises**
foreign exchange warrant

**warrant obligataire**
debt warrant

*Terminología de empréstitos y préstamos*

*Español*—Inglés

## - A -

**acción al portador**
transferable share

**acción de primera clase**
blue chip

**acción de usufructo**
dividend-right share

**acción gratuita**
bonus share

**acción negociable**
transferable share

**acción transferible**
transferable share

**acciones con derecho a dividendo**
dividend stock

**acciones de garantía**
qualification stock

**acciones nominativas**
registered stock; personal stock

**acciones ordinarias**
common stock

**acciones pagadas**
paid-up stock; fully paid stock

**acciones preferenciales, preferentes, preferidas**
preferred stock

**acciones preferenciales, (preferentes, preferidas) acumuladas**
cumulative preferred stock

**acciones privilegiadas**
debenture stock [U.S.]

**aceptación bancaria**
banker's acceptance

**activo neto**
stockholders' equity; shareholders' equity; owners' equity; equity; net worth; shareholders' funds [U.K.]

**acuerdo de compensación**
clearing agreement

**acuerdo de recompra**
repurchase agreement (RP; repos); system repurchase agreement

**acuerdo de retención de acciones**
share-retention agreement [IFC]

**acumulación (de vencimientos)**
bunching (of maturities)

**adjudicación a precio uniforme**
Dutch auction [U.S.]

**afinamiento (de la economía)**
fine-tuning (of the economy)

**agente de bolsa**
dealer [stock market]

**agente (de cambio y bolsa)**
broker

**agente de contrapartida**
dealer [options market]

**agente financiero**
fiscal agent

**agente pagador**
paying agent

**agente vendedor**
sales agent [securities]

**agio**
agio; premium [securities]

**agiotista**
jobber; market maker

**amortización**
amortization

**ampliación del capital**
capital widening

**analista de valores**
securities analyst

**anticipos sin garantía escrita**
clean advances

**anuncio de emisión efectuada**
tombstone

**anuncio preliminar de una nueva emisión**
red herring

**arbitraje**
arbitrage; switch

**arbitraje en el tiempo**
time arbitrage

**arbitraje espacial**
two-point arbitrage; space arbitrage

**arbitrajista**
arbitrageur

**asentamiento**
shake-out (of the market)

**atracción**
crowding-in

**aumento del capital con respecto al trabajo**
capital deepening

**autorización permanente**
shelf registration

**aval**
aval

## - B -

**banco agente**
agent bank

**banco codirector, coadministrador**
comanager; colead manager

**banco comercial**
chartered bank; commercial bank; clearing bank [U.K.]

**banco con autorización federal**
federally chartered bank [U.S.]

**banco corresponsal**
agent bank

**banco de inversiones**
investment bank [U.S.]; merchant bank [U.K.]

**banco director**
lead bank; lead manager

**banco extraterritorial**
offshore bank

**banco fiduciario**
trust bank (Shintaku Ginko) [Japan]

**banco múltiple**
combined commercial and investment bank; multibank; all-purpose bank

**bancos establecidos en las principales plazas financieras**
money-center banks

**base de capital**
capital base

**bono**
bond

**bono ajustable, indizado**
indexed bond; index-linked bond

**bono al portador**
bearer bond

**bono amortiguador**
cushion bond

**bono "bulldog"**
Bulldog bond

**bono clásico**
straight bond

**bono comerciable**
marketable bond

**bono con certificado**
warrant bond

**bono (con clasificación) AAA**
AAA bond

**bono con cupón**
coupon(-bearing) bond

**bono con garantía de activos**
debenture (bond)

**bono con interés variable**
floating-rate bond

**bono con opción de cambio de divisa**
multiple (currency) option bond

**bono con tipo de interés renovable**
roly-poly bond

**bono con tipos de interés escalonados (fijados anticipadamente)**
stepped-rate bond

**bono con vencimiento elegido a la suerte**
serial bond, loan

**bono de ahorro**
savings bond [France, Belgium, U.S.]

**bono de calidad bancaria**
bank quality bond

**bono de descuento intensivo**
deep-discount bond, note

**bono de primer orden, de primera clase**
top-rated bond

**bono de una empresa privada, de una compaña, de una sociedad anónima**
corporate bond

**bono de usufructo**
dividend-right certificate

**bono de vencimiento ajustable**
extendible bond; extendible maturity bond

**bono de vencimiento escalonado**
serial bond, loan

**bono de venta continua**
bond sold on tap

**bono del Tesoro**
Treasury bond [U.S.]

**bono del Tesoro (EE.UU.) a muy corto plazo**
cash-management bill

**bono descontado**
discount bond

**bono emitido con descuento**
original-issue discount bond

**bono hipotecario**
mortgage bond

**bono negociable**
marketable bond

**bono no comerciable**
nonmarketable bond

**bono no negociable**
nonmarketable bond

**bono no rescatable, no redimible antes del vencimiento**
noncallable bond

**bono ordinario**
straight bond

**bono pagadero con los ingresos (del proyecto)**
revenue bond

**bono participatorio**
income bond; participating bond

**bono perpetuo**
nonmaturing, nonredeemable government bond; perpetual bond; consol [U.K.]

**bono perpetuo, de renta vitalicia**
annuity bond

**bono redimible con descuento antes de su vencimiento**
accreted call bond

**bono rescatable, redimible antes del vencimiento**
callable bond

**bono retractable**
retractable, putable bond

**bono samurai**
Samurai bond

**bono sin cupón**
zero-coupon bond

**bono sin garantía específica**
debenture (bond)

**bono yanqui**
Yankee bond

**bonos de responsabilidad general**
general obligations; general obligation bonds

**bonos del Gobierno británico**
gilt-edged securities

## - C -

**cajero automático, permanente**
automatic teller machine

**calendario de emisiones**
issuing calendar

**cámara de compensación**
clearing house

**capital accionario**
equity capital; capital stock (of a corporation)

**capital de riesgo**
risk capital

**capital social**
equity capital; capital stock (of a corporation)

**capitales itinerantes**
hot money; funk money

**capitalización**
capitalization

**carta de seguridades**
letter of comfort

**cartera de acciones**
shareownership

**cartera de préstamos**
loan portfolio

**cartera líquida**
liquidity portfolio

**casa de aceptaciones**
acceptance, accepting house

**casa de descuento**
discount house; bill broker

**cédula hipotecaria**
mortgage bond

**centésimo de punto porcentual**
basis point

**certificado de adeudo**
debt certificate

**certificado de depositario**
depositary receipt

**certificado de depósito**
certificate of deposit (CD)

**certificado de depósito con tipo de interés renovable**
roll-over certificate of deposit; roly-poly certificate of deposit

**certificado de depósito de tramo**
tranche certificate of deposit

**certificado de depósito de US$100.000 o más**
jumbo certificate of deposit

**certificado de depósito negociable**
negotiable time certificate of deposit

**certificado de depósito sin límite, de libre compra**
straight, tap certificate of deposit

**certificado de participación**
participation certificate

**certificado de solvencia**
soundness certificate

**certificado de transferencia de préstamos**
pass-through certificate; participation certificate

**certificado en divisas**
foreign exchange warrant

**certificado nominativo**
bond certificate

**certificado para compra de bonos**
debt warrant

**certificado para la compra de acciones, bonos**
warrant

**certificado para la compra de pagarés del Tesoro**
warrant into government securities (WINGS)

**certificado provisional**
scrip certificate; bearer scrip

**certificado separable**
detachable warrant

**cheque de banco**
banker's draft

**clasificar**
rate, to; grade, to

**cláusula de disponibilidad**
switch, availability clause

**cláusula de obligación negativa**
negative pledge clause

**cláusula de revisión**
trigger clause [IBRD]

**cláusula de salvaguardia**
jeopardy clause; disaster clause; break clause

**cláusula *pari passu***
pari passu clause

**cláusula recíproca en caso de incumplimiento**
cross-default clause

**cobertura del servicio de la deuda**
debt-service coverage

**coeficiente de costo en recursos internos**
domestic resource cost ratio

**coeficiente de endeudamiento [Esp.]**
debt-equity ratio; debt-to-equity ratio

**coeficiente de explotación**
working ratio

**coeficiente de operación**
operating ratio

**coeficiente de solvencia [Esp.]**
current ratio; working-capital ratio

**coeficiente neto de explotación**
operating ratio

**coeficientes de liquidez**
liquidity ratios

**colocación en el mercado secundario**
secondary offering

**colocación especial**
special placement

**colocación privada**
private placement

**colocación pública**
public offering (of shares)

**comisión de administración**
management fee

**comisión de garantía**
guarantee commission, fee [IBRD]; underwriting fee

**comisión de gestión**
agency fee [Euromarket]; management fee

**comisión de participación**
participation fee

**comisión de renegociación**
extension fee

**comisión de suscripción**
underwriting fee

**comisión de ventas**
selling fee [Euromarket]

**comisión inicial**
front-end fee

**comisión por compromiso, por inmovilización de fondos**
commitment fee; stand-by fee

**compañía comisionada**
commissioned company [Japan]

**compañía de capitales de riesgo**
venture capital company

**compañía de inversiones**
investment company, fund

**compensación de débitos y créditos**
multilateral netting

**compra en descubierto**
margin buying [stock exchange]

**compra y venta simultánea**
matched sale-purchase transaction

**compromiso de compra y reventa**
purchase and resale agreement [Canada]

**compromisos por países**
country exposure

**concertar un préstamo a través de un consorcio (bancario, de financiamiento)**
syndicate, to (a loan)

**condonación (de una deuda)**
cancellation (of a debt)

**congelación del interés en un nivel mínimo (cuando la tasa de mercado desciende a menos de ese nivel)**
drop lock

**consorcio (bancario)**
selling consortium, group, syndicate [Euromarket]

**consorcio (bancario, de financiamiento)**
syndicate

**consorcio de suscriptores**
underwriting consortium, group, syndicate

**"contango"**
contango

**contrato de compra garantizada**
take-and-pay contract

**contrato firme de compra (sin derecho de rescisión)**
take-or-pay contract

**corredor**
sales agent [securities]

**corredor de bolsa**
dealer [stock market]

**corredor de bolsa independiente**
floor trader

**corredor (de cambio, de bolsa)**
broker

**corredor de inversiones**
investment broker

**corredor de valores**
securities dealer; securities firm

**corredor de valores del Estado**
government security dealer

**corredor (mercado primario)**
primary dealer

**corretaje**
brokerage

**corriente de fondos**
funds flow; flow of funds

**costo de los empréstitos con doble ponderación**
double-weighted borrowing cost [IBRD]

**costo en recursos internos**
domestic resource cost (DRC)

**cotización**
fixing

**cotizar**
post, to (a rate)

**crédito autoamortizable**
self-liquidating credit

**crédito con garantía de otro crédito**
back-to-back (loan, borrowing)

**crédito garantizado por el Estado**
sovereign credit

**crédito recíproco**
swap (transaction)

**crédito renovable, refinanciable**
roll-over credit

**crédito rotatorio, renovable**
revolving credit

**cuadro de corrientes financieras**
flow-of-fund table [national accounts]

**cuarto mercado**
fourth market

**cuasibanco**
near-bank [Canada]

**cuasidinero**
near-money; quasi-money

**cuenta corriente del Tesoro**
Treasury tax and loan account [U.S.]

**cuenta corriente que devenga intereses**
negotiable order of withdrawal (NOW) account

**cuenta de administración de fondos**
cash-management account

**cuenta de anticipos**
imprest account, fund

**cuenta de primas de emisión**
share-premium account [IFC]

**cupón**
coupon

**curva de rendimiento**
yield curve

## - D -

**debenture**
debenture (bond)

**departamento bancario considerado como extraterritorial**
offshore banking unit (OBU)

**departamentos fiduciarios de bancos**
bank trust departments

**depósitos bancarios**
bank money

**depreciación**
amortization

**derecho**
right (to purchase shares)

**derecho (del accionista)**
corporate right

**derecho de suscripción**
subscription right

**descontar**
discount, to

**descubierto**
uncovered; naked

**descuento**
discount [bills]; markdown [foreign exchange]

**descuento de conversión**
conversion discount

**descuento de pagarés a mediano plazo**
forfeiting

**descuento impositivo**
tax credit

**descuento sin recurso**
discount without recourse

**descuento sobre el valor a la par**
discount from par [securities market]

**desintermediación**
disintermediation

**desplazamiento**
crowding-out

**deuda consolidada**
funded debt

**deuda prioritaria**
senior debt

**deuda subordinada**
junior debt; subordinated debt

**diferencia**
spread

**diferencial**
spread

**dinero a la vista**
call money; day-to-day money; demand money; money at call

**dinero en el sentido estricto**
narrow money

**dinero en sentido amplio**
broad money

**dinero exigible**
call money; day-to-day money; demand money; money at call

**disagio**
disagio

**distribución**
allotment

**dividendo en acciones**
stock dividend

**división de acciones**
split; split-up

## - E -

**efecto a la vista o de vencimiento a muy corto plazo**
hot bill

**efecto carrusel**
merry-go-round effect

**efecto comercial**
trade bill [U.K.]

**efectos a corto plazo**
short-term paper

**efectos comerciales en eurodivisas**
Eurocommercial paper

**efectos comerciales**
commercial paper; commercial bills

**efectos en cobro, cobranza**
float [banking]

**efectos privados**
private paper

**efectos públicos**
government paper

**elasticidad tributaria global**
tax buoyancy

**emisión adquirida anticipadamente por un consorcio bancario**
bought deal

**emisión atascada**
hung-up issue

**emisión continua**
tap issue

**emisión de bonos en el exterior**
external bond issue

**emisión de valores de capital**
capital issue

**emisión empantanada**
hung-up issue

**emisión exploratoria**
red herring issue

**emisiones de organismos federales**
agency securities, obligations

**emisor**
issuer

**empréstito de contrapartida**
back-to-back (loan, borrowing)

**empréstito de suma alzada**
lump-sum borrowing [IFC]

**empréstitos calificados**
qualified borrowings [IBRD]

**empréstitos de referencia**
proxy borrowing [IBRD]

**empréstitos gigantescos**
jumbo borrowing

**encaje legal adicional**
marginal reserve requirement

**esquela**
tombstone

**estado de flujo de fondos**
statement of changes in financial position; source and application of funds statement; funds statement; source and use of funds statement; funds flow statement; changes in working capital statement

**eurobono**
Eurobond

**eurocrédito**
Eurocredit

**eurodivisas**
Eurocurrency

**eurodólar**
Eurodollar

**euromercado**
Euromarket

**euromoneda**
Euromoney

**europréstamo**
Euroloan

**evaluación actuarial**
actuarial evaluation

**evaluar**
rate, to; grade, to

**exceso de oferta**
overhang

**expectativas racionales**
rational expectations

## - F -

**factor de ajuste para fines de amortización**
amortization adjustment factor [currency pool]

**factor de revaluación**
revaluation factor [currency pool]

**facultad para contraer compromisos**
commitment authority

**fecha de desembolso**
payout date

**fecha de valor**
value date

**fijación de precios abierta**
open pricing

**financiamiento con garantía de contratos**
contract financing

**financiamiento con recurso limitado**
limited recourse finance

**financiamiento concatenado**
piggy-back financing

**financiamiento conjunto**
joint financing

**financiamiento de los últimos vencimientos**
funding latter maturities [IBRD]

**financiamiento en condiciones de mercado**
market-related lending

**financiamiento innovador**
creative financing

**financiamiento paralelo**
parallel financing

**financiamiento sin posibilidad de recurso**
nonrecourse finance

**flotación impura, dirigida**
dirty float

**flotación limpia**
clean float

**fluctuación de los tipos de interés debida a la fuga de capitales**
interest leakage

**flujo de fondos**
funds flow; flow of funds

**fondo común de inversiones**
money-market (mutual) fund; mutual fund

**fondo común de monedas**
currency pool

**fondo de amortización**
sinking fund

**fondo de anticipos**
imprest account, fund

**fondo de inversión que cobra una comisión**
load fund

**fondo de inversión que no cobra una comisión**
no-load fund

**fondo de inversiones**
investment company, fund

**fondo mutuo**
money market (mutual) fund; mutual fund

**fondo rotatorio**
revolving fund

**fondos comprados**
purchased funds

**fondos de reserva para redención de capital accionario**
capital redemption reserve funds

**fondos de un día para otro**
overnight funds

**fondos federales**
federal funds

**formación de un consorcio (bancario, de financiamiento)**
syndication

**freno fiscal**
fiscal drag

**futuros**
futures [commodities market]

## - G -

**ganancia bruta en cuenta de valores**
securities margin account

**ganancias no realizadas**
unrealized gains

**garantía**
guarantee [IBRD]

**garantía (dada por terceros)**
comfort

**garantía (del Estado)**
guarantee

**gasto concentrado al comienzo de un período**
front-loaded spending

**Gensaki**
Gensaki

**gestión de caja, de liquidez**
cash management

**gestión del pasivo**
liability management

**gran banco**
city bank

**grupo de colocación**
selling consortium, group, syndicate [Euromarket]

**grupo de dirección**
management, managing group [Eurodollar market]

**grupo de suscripción**
underwriting consortium, group, syndicate

**grupo garante**
underwriting consortium, group, syndicate

**grupo vendedor**
selling consortium, group, syndicate [Euromarket]

## - H -

**honorario del banco director**
praecipium; praecipuum

## - I -

**inflación básica**
core inflation

**instrumento negociable**
negotiable instrument

**instrumentos**
instruments

**instrumentos de la deuda pública**
government debt instruments

**instrumentos financieros a plazo**
financial futures

**intensificación financiera**
financial deepening

**intercambio de deudas**
debt-for-debt swap

**intercambio de monedas**
currency swap; swap (transaction)

**interés de "contango"**
contango rate; continuation rate

**interés mayoritario**
proprietary interest

**interés nominal**
coupon rate

**interés nominal corriente**
current coupon (rate)

**intermediación**
intermediation

**intermediario financiero**
financial intermediary

**inversión orientada a aumentar la eficiencia de la producción y reducir los costos**
capital-deepening investment

**inversión periódica de monto constante**
averaging

## - L -

**lastre fiscal**
fiscal drag

**letra a cierto plazo de la fecha de presentación**
after-sight bill

**letra aduanera garantizada**
custom-duty bill

**letra bancaria**
bank bill

**letra comercial**
trade bill [U.K.]

**letra de banco**
banker's draft

**letra de cambio**
bill of exchange

**LIBOR**
LIBOR (London Interbank Offered Rate)

**librador (p. ej. de un pagaré)**
maker (e.g., of a note)

**libranza en divisas**
foreign exchange warrant

**límites legales (de las compras en descubierto)**
margin requirements [stock exchange]

**línea de crédito de apoyo**
back-up line of credit

**lista de acciones con sus cotizaciones**
share list

**lista de espera**
queue

## - M -

**M1**
M1

**M2**
M2

**M3**
M3

**manipulación de la contabilidad (para aparentar una mejor situación)**
window dressing

**margen**
spread

**memorando de información**
placement memorandum; placing memorandum

**memorando de oferta**
offering memorandum

**mercado a plazo, a término, de futuros**
forward market

**mercado abierto**
open market

**mercado al contado**
spot market; cash market

**mercado basado en el prestigio de los prestatarios**
name market

**mercado de capitales**
capital market

**mercado de corto plazo**
short-term paper market

**mercado de productos disponibles, de entrega inmediata**
spot market [commodities]

**mercado de títulos al portador**
bearer market

**mercado extrabursátil**
over-the-counter market (OTC)

**mercado financiero**
open market

**mercado fuera de bolsa**
over-the-counter market (OTC); third market; off-the-board market

**mercado gris**
grey, gray market

**mercado inmovilizado**
locked market

**mercado paralelo**
parallel market

**mercado primario, de emisión**
primary market

**mercado secundario**
secondary market

**multibanco**
combined commercial and investment bank; multibank; all-purpose bank

## - N -

**nivel de endeudamiento relativo al capital**
leverage (ratio) [U.S.]; gearing (ratio) [U.K.]

**no cotizado en la bolsa**
unlisted (security)

## - O -

**obligación**
bond

**obligación al portador**
bearer bond

**obligación (con clasificación) AAA**
AAA bond

**obligación contingente**
contingent obligation [IBRD]

**oferta pública**
public offering (of shares)

**oferta pública de compra**
take-over bid

**opción**
option

**opción de cambio de divisa**
multicurrency option

**opción de compra**
call option

**opción de compra de acciones**
stock option

**opción de compra de bonos con rendimiento inferior al del bono inicial**
out-of-(the)-money option

**opción de financiamiento residual**
take-over option [IBRD]

**opción de venta**
put option

**opción de venta y compra**
straddle; call-and-put option

**operación de cobertura por venta a plazo**
short hedge

**operaciones de cobertura por compra a plazo**
long hedge

**operaciones de cobertura, de protección cambiaria**
hedging

**orden de compra**
trading ticket [securities]

**orden de venta**
trading ticket [securities]

**organismo de clasificación de valores**
rating agency

## - P -

**pagaré**
note; promissory note

**pagaré a corto plazo**
short-term note

**pagaré a corto plazo en espera de ingresos no tributarios**
revenue-anticipation note (RAN)

**pagaré a corto plazo para financiar un proyecto**
project note

**pagaré al portador**
bearer note

**pagaré bancario**
bank bill

**pagaré con cupón**
coupon note

**pagaré con interés variable**
floating-rate note (IRN)

**pagaré con tipo de interés flotante perpetuo**
perpetual floating-rate note

**pagaré de vencimiento ajustable**
extendible note; extendible maturity note

**pagaré del Tesoro**
Treasury note [U.S.]

**pagaré del Tesoro a corto plazo**
Treasury bill [U.S.]

**pagaré descontado**
discount note

**pagaré en previsión de una emisión de bonos**
bond-anticipation note (BAN)

**pagaré respaldado por ingresos fiscales previstos**
tax-anticipation note (TAN)

**pagarés descontados consolidados**
consolidated discount notes

**pagarés que devengan intereses**
interest-bearing notes

**papel a corto plazo**
short-term paper

**papel comercial**
commercial paper; commercial bills

**participación de fundador**
founder's share

**participación en el capital social**
equity ownership

**participación en una sociedad**
partnership share

**participación proporcional**
funding pro rata [IBRD]

**participación sin posibilidad de recurso**
nonrecourse participation

**pase financiero**
swap (transaction)

**patrimonio**
stockholders' equity; shareholders' equity; owners' equity; equity; net worth; shareholders' funds [U.K.]

**patrimonio neto**
stockholders' equity; shareholders' equity; owners' equity; equity net worth; shareholders' funds [U.K.]

**perfil general del financiamiento**
overall risk profile [IBRD]

**período "after-market"**
after-market

**período de pago**
payment period [IBRD]

**período de prohibición de rescate**
noncall period

**petrobono**
petrobond

**posición de venta en descubierto**
short position

**praecipuum**
praecipium; praecipuum

**precio**
price (of a bond)

**precio comprador**
bid price; buying rate [securities market]

**precio de compra**
bid price

**precio de conversión**
conversion price

**precio de cuenta**
accounting price

**precio de mercado**
arm's length (price)

**precio de transferencia interna**
transfer price

**precio de venta**
selling rate

**precio económico**
economic price; efficiency price

**precio en la frontera**
border price

**precio fijado en contrato (para ejercitar una opción de compra)**
striking price; exercise price

**precio fronterizo**
border price

**precio mínimo en subasta a la baja**
stop-out price

**precio neto**
payout price

**precio vendedor**
ask(ed) price [securities market]; selling rate

**prestamista de última instancia**
lender of last resort

**préstamo "A"**
"A" loan

**préstamo a la vista**
call loan

**préstamo a mediano o largo plazo**
term loan

**préstamo amortizable en su mayor parte al vencimiento**
balloon loan

**préstamo "B"**
"B" loan

**préstamo "balloon"**
balloon loan

**préstamo cofinanciado**
coloan

**préstamo con intermediación de un banco**
back-to-back (loan, borrowing)

**préstamo concedido por un club bancario, por un consorcio**
club loan

**préstamo de títulos con garantía en efectivo**
cash security loan

**préstamo de un consorcio**
syndicated loan

**préstamo en pirámide, en cascada**
apex loan

**préstamo en valores**
security lending [IBRD]

**préstamo en valores garantizado por otro(s) valor(es)**
borrow-pledge security loan

**préstamo incluido en el sistema de fondo común de monedas**
pooled loan

**préstamo que se halla en dificultades**
distressed loan

**préstamo reajustado**
indexed loan [currency pool]

**préstamo reembolsable de una sola vez a su vencimiento**
bullet issue

**préstamo subordinado**
subordinated loan

**préstamos cruzados en divisas**
back-to-back (loan, borrowing)

**préstamos pendientes**
exposure

**prestatario preferencial, preferente, de primera clase**
prime borrower; premier borrower

**prima**
premium [foreign exchange; option market; securities]

**prima de conversión**
conversion premium

**prima de emisión**
premium [stocks]

**prima de liquidez**
liquidity premium

**prima de rescate**
call premium

**prima pagada por aplazamiento de entrega**
backwardation

**prima por inflación**
inflation premium

**prima por riesgo**
risk premium

**promedio móvil (ponderado)**
running (weighted) average

**prospecto**
prospectus

**protección contra rescate anticipado**
call protection

**protección de "swap" doble**
cross-currency interest hedge; double-hedge swap

**punto de equilibrio**
break-even point [stock market]

## - R -

**recompra**
buy-back [Canada]

**recompra de divisas en moneda nacional**
inward swap

**redescontar**
rediscount

**redescontar con compromiso de reventa**
take in, to (bills)

**redescuento**
discount window

**reembolso en cuotas iguales**
level repayment

**refinanciamiento**
roll-over

**refinanciamiento anticipado**
advanced refunding

**refinanciamiento de monto igual**
even roll

**relación activo disponible-pasivo corriente**
acid-test, liquid, quick ratio

**relación corriente [América latina]**
current ratio; working-capital ratio

**relación de Bruno**
Bruno ratio

**relación de cobertura de intereses**
interest-coverage ratio

**relación de cuenta**
accounting ratio

**relación de endeudamiento**
debt ratio

**relación de endeudamiento a largo plazo**
long-term debt ratio

**relación del servicio de la deuda**
debt-service ratio

**relación derivada del balance general**
balance-sheet ratio

**relación deuda-capital**
debt-equity ratio; debt-to-equity ratio

**relación endeudamiento/capital propio**
leverage (ratio); gearing (ratio)

**relación precio-utilidades**
price/earnings ratio (P/E ratio; PER)

**relación préstamos desembolsados y pendientes—capital y reservas**
gearing ratio

**relaciones de actividad**
activity ratios

**relaciones de gestión**
operating ratios

**relaciones de liquidez**
liquidity ratios

**relaciones de rentabilidad**
profitability ratios; revenue-covenant ratios

**relaciones financieras**
financial ratios

**rémora fiscal**
fiscal drag

**rendimiento al vencimiento**
yield to maturity (YTM)

**rendimiento equivalente a un interés nominal**
coupon equivalent yield

**renovación**
roll-over

**renunciar a una garantía**
take out, to [IBRD]

**represión financiera**
financial repression

**représtamo**
onlending

**resquicio**
window (in a market)

**reutilización de las ganancias**
roll-over of gains

**reventa de divisas en moneda nacional**
outward swap

**riesgo**
exposure

**riesgo de liquidez**
cash risk; liquid-holdings risk

**riesgo que plantea el país**
sovereign risk

**riesgo relacionado con el refinanciamiento**
refinancing risk [IBRD]

**riesgo relacionado con el margen**
spread risk [IBRD]

**riesgo relacionado con los tipos de interés**
interest-rate risk

**riesgo relacionado con un desfase**
lag risk [IBRD]; mismatch risk [IBRD]

**riesgo soberano**
sovereign risk

**riesgos de refinanciamiento**
roll-over risks

## - S -

**sacudimiento**
shake-out (of the market)

**saldo que pasa (al ejercicio siguiente)**
carry-over

**sector**
segment; sector (of the market)

**segmento**
segment; sector (of the market)

**servicio bancario internacional**
international banking facility (IBF)

**sin garantía escrita**
clean

**sin intereses**
flat

**sistema de fondo común de monedas**
currency pooling system

**sistema de la Reserva Federal**
Federal Reserve System [U.S.]

**sistema de tipos de interés basados en una "cesta" de empréstitos pendientes**
pool-based lending rate system [IBRD]

**situación en que el precio al contado es superior al precio a plazo**
backwardation

**sociedad comisionada**
commissioned company

**sociedad de inversión con número de acciones fijo**
closed-end (investment) fund

**sociedad de inversiones**
investment company, fund

**sociedad de inversiones con número de acciones variable**
open-end (investment) fund; unit trust [U.K.]

**sociedad de valores**
securities dealer; securities firm

**solvencia**
credit standing; creditworthiness

**solvencia crediticia**
credit standing; creditworthiness

**subasta a la baja**
Dutch auction

**subcuenta de endeudamiento del prestatario**
borrower's indebtedness subaccount [currency pool]

**subpréstamo**
subloan

**subprestatario**
subborrower

**swap**
swap (transaction)

## - T -

**tasa crítica de rentabilidad**
hurdle rate

**tasa de activación**
trigger rate

**tasa de actualización**
discount rate

**tasa de actualización de equilibrio**
cross-over discount rate; equalizing discount rate

**tasa de inmovilización**
lock rate

**tasa de interés de cuenta (TIC)**
accounting rate of interest (ARI)

**tasa de interés del consumo (TICO)**
consumption rate of interest (CRI)

**tasa de interés real**
real interest rate

**tasa de los fondos federales**
federal funds rate

**tasa preferencial**
prime rate

**tenedor de bonos**
bondholder

**tercer mercado**
third market; off-the-board market

**tipo de cambio mínimo**
floor rate of exchange

**tipo de interés de cuenta (TIC)**
accounting rate of interest (ARI)

**tipo de interés del consumo (TICO)**
consumption rate of interest (CRI)

**tipo de interés pagado por aplazamiento de entrega**
backwardation rate

**tipo de interés para préstamos a la vista**
call-money rate

**tipo de interés real**
real interest rate

**tipo de interés variable basado en una "cesta" de empréstitos pendientes**
pool-based variable lending rate [IBRD]

**tipo de los fondos federales**
federal funds rate

**tipo de redescuento**
discount rate

**tipo Lombard**
Lombard rate [Federal Republic of Germany]

**tipo para préstamos con garantía de valores**
broker loan rate

**tipo preferencial**
prime rate

**título**
security

**título al portador**
bearer security

**título consistente en un asiento bancario**
book-entry security

**título hipotecario**
mortgage bond

**título provisional**
scrip certificate; bearer scrip

**títulos con cupón**
coupon paper

**títulos de organismos federales**
agency securities, obligations

**traducción de monedas**
currency translation

**transacción de vencimientos simultáneos**
matched-maturity transaction [IBRD]

**transacción ficticia**
wash sale

**transacciones de personas iniciadas**
inside, insider dealing

**transferencia electrónica de fondos**
electronic funds transfer (EFT)

**transformación (bancaria)**
transformation

**trueque de bonos de valor nominal igual**
even par swap

**trueque de tipos de interés**
interest-rate swap

## - U -

**unidad de cuenta europea (UCE)**
European Unit of Account (EUA)

**unidad monetaria europea (ECU)**
European Currency Unit (ECU)

**utilidades no distribuidas**
retained earnings

## - V -

**valor**
security

**valor con tipo de interés descendente**
step-down (security)

**valor contable, en libros**
book value

**valor cotizado en bolsa**
listed security

**valor crítico**
switching value

**valor de conversión**
conversion value

**valor de primera clase**
blue chip

**valor de protección**
hedge

**valor en venta continua**
tap security

**valor nominal**
full face value; par value; face value

**valor precursor de tendencias**
bellwether security

**valores a corto plazo**
short-term paper

**valores de inversión a largo plazo**
investment securities

**valores de primer orden**
gilt-edged securities

**venta de un crédito fuera del consorcio**
sell-down

**venta en descubierto**
short sale

**venta sin compromiso de garantía de emisión**
best efforts sale

**ventanilla automática**
automatic teller machine (ATM)

## - W -

**"warrant" en divisas**
foreign exchange warrant

**"warrant" para compra de bonos**
debt warrant

**"warrant" separable**
detachable warrant

## - Z -

**zona bancaria franca**
offshore banking center